Textbook

American Red Cross
Basic Water Safety

ISBN: 0-86536-141-X

Acknowledgments

The Lifesaving Revision Advisory Committee of the American Red Cross provided the primary advice and guidance for the design and content of Basic Water Safety and Emergency Water Safety. The members of the committee included:

Reverend Rodney P. Bourg, St. Bernard Parish Chapter, Chalmette, Louisiana.

Paul M. Cerio, Supervisor of Aquatics, University of Nebraska, Omaha, Nebraska.

Darwin DeLappa, Director, Water Safety, NYS Parks, Recreation and Historic Preservation, Albany, New York.

Michael C. Giles, Aquatics Director, University of Southern Mississippi, Hattiesburg, Mississippi.

Ralph Johnson, Ph.D., Associate Professor, Indiana University of Pennsylvania, Indiana, Pennsylvania.

John Malatak, Officer, Health and Safety, American Red Cross, National Headquarters, Washington, D.C.

Jane W. McCharen, Metro Public Schools, Nashville, Tennessee.

Mike Miller, Director of Aquatics, University of Missouri, Kansas City, Missouri.

Kathryn Scott, Department of Physical Education, University of California at Berkeley, Berkeley, California.

Michael T. Shellito, Department of Parks and Recreation, City of Roseville, Roseville, California.

Marilyn Strom, Aquatics Director, University of Massachusetts-Boston, Boston, Massachusetts.

Royce Van Evera, Director of Community Services, American Red Cross, Albany Area Chapter, Albany, New York.

Lelia Vaughan, Recreation and Park Consultant, Jonesville, Texas

Members of the development team at the American Red Cross national headquarters included: Frank Carroll; Jon Martindale; Lawrence Newell, Ed.D.; and Thomas C. Werts.

The following locations participated in field tests of Basic Water Safety and Emergency Water Safety: Ashtabula, Ohio; Tampa, Florida; Providence, Rhode Island; South Bend, Indiana; Wichita, Kansas; Sacramento, California; Pasadena, California; Houston, Texas; Nashville, Tennessee; Omaha, Nebraska; Milwaukee, Wisconsin; Salt Lake City, Utah; Palo Alto, California; Greenville, South Carolina; Boston, Massachusetts; and Santa Ana, California.

Contents

Contents

Introduction

Since 1914, the American Red Cross has conducted a water safety program to develop safety skills and knowledge for safety in, on, and around the water.

No one knows how many lives have been saved or accidents prevented because of this program, but there is no question that this program, together with the efforts of other agencies, has helped cut the drowning rate in this country from 10.4 drownings per 100,000 population in 1914 to fewer than 3 drownings per 100,000 population in recent years.

Unfortunately, too many people lack the knowledge and skill necessary to recognize hazardous conditions or practices, or to safely get themselves or someone else out of danger. Swimming and water safety instruction continue to be the most fundamental part of the American Red Cross water safety program.

The purpose of the Basic Water Safety course and this textbook is to provide individuals and families with general water safety information. By creating an awareness of how accidents happen and how to prevent them, swimmers and nonswimmers in this course will develop a desire to be safe. They, in turn, will contribute to widespread healthful and safe aquatic recreation.

The glossary will be helpful to you to understand the terms used in this textbook and in *Emergency Water Safety.*

1 *Preventing Water Accidents*

Case History

Proper supervision at swimming areas is critical to preventing water accidents. The following case history shows why:

A group of children were standing on a dock at a lake, waiting to be taken for a boat ride. They began to push each other playfully, and some ended up in the water.

One 10-year-old boy fell in but couldn't swim. The other children saw his arms flailing and bubbles rising in the water. When the counselors were informed, two of them searched the water but found nothing, while a third counted the children at the scene.

Water rescue personnel arrived at the dock area, and the boy's body was recovered. There were reports later that the counselors themselves had participated in the horseplay that caused the accident.

The children should have been instructed to play a safe distance from the water. If they came too close to the water, the counselors should have moved them away.

What Causes Water Accidents?

Most of us find water recreation relaxing and enjoyable. Even though the human body is not adapted to breathing naturally in water, we learn how to wade and play, and many of us are quite good at swimming.

Yet we know that there are limits to what we can do safely and that there are dangers in the water, even in swimming pools.

According to the National Safety Council, about 6,000 Americans drown every year. Only motor vehicle accidents and falls cause more accidental deaths than drowning. Drowning can be the result of boating accidents, carelessness on the part of swimmers, or accidental falls into the water. Many drowning victims are reported to have been good swimmers.

Major Causes of Drownings and Dangerous Accidents
- Alcohol and drug use while participating in water recreation
- Diving into unknown waters or water that is too shallow
- Overestimation of ability and stamina
- Sudden immersion
- Accidents involving small boats
- Medical emergencies, such as heart attacks and seizures

Alcohol and Drug Use While Participating in Water Recreation
The U.S. Coast Guard warns that drinking alcohol or using drugs—
- Can make your reaction time slower than normal.
- Can make it hard for you to decide what to do.
- Can make dangerous situations seem less threatening, so you're more likely to take foolish chances.
- Can make you more susceptible to accidents, injury, and drowning.

Because alcohol and drug use contribute to danger, it's best to stay sober and free of drugs.

Diving Into Unknown Waters or Water That Is Too Shallow
If you dive without first checking the underwater area or you dive into water that is too shallow, you risk striking an underwater object or hitting the bottom. This can cause a spinal injury, one of the most severe injuries resulting from water accidents. A spinal injury can mean temporary or permanent paralysis and even death.

Overestimation of Ability and Stamina
The "dangerous too's"—swimming *too* long or *too* far away, staying *too* long in cold water or on a sunny beach, and playing *too* hard—can put you in a potentially dangerous situation. Many people, particularly younger and less experienced swimmers, push their limits while in or around the water and then get into trouble.

Sudden Immersion
In recent years, well over half of drowning victims in the United States were doing something other than swimming or playing in the water, according to the National Safety Council. Victims fell into the water from docks, bridges, and shores; they were involved in recreational or commercial boating accidents; or they had accidents in the home or at workplaces near water.

Sudden immersion can also occur when someone is wading and steps into an unexpected drop-off where the water is deep.

Accidents Involving Small Boats
The National Safety Council reports that more than 90 percent of the drownings from boating accidents involve occupants of small boats. In many cases the boaters were untrained and inexperienced, had been drinking, and were not wearing personal flotation devices (PFDs).

Medical Emergencies
Medical problems, such as heart attacks and epileptic seizures, cause some drownings and near-drownings. Tragically, other swimmers often do not recognize that a heart attack or seizure victim is having a medical emergency until it's too late to help.

In, on, or around the water, many lives could be saved if we all worked harder to prevent accidents and to prepare for emergencies.

Before You Swim

The following is a list of safety steps that you should take prior to participating in aquatic activities. This course will teach you many of these steps. But if you want to learn more, you should enroll in other American Red Cross Health and Safety courses.
- Take time to learn about swimming, boating, and first aid.
- Have an emergency plan for responding to water accidents, whatever your level of swimming skill.
- Choose a safe place for water recreation.
- Use Coast Guard–approved PFDs.
- Check out potential water hazards.
- Know local weather conditions.
- Know what to do for cramps, sunburn, heat stroke, and heat exhaustion.
- Avoid hyperventilation.
- Dress appropriately.
- Take time to think how to help yourself safely in an emergency.
- Take time to think how to help others safely in an emergency.

Take Time to Learn More

Take the time to learn all you can about swimming, boating, and first aid. You've made a good start by taking this Basic Water Safety course.

To find out about other classes and courses, check with schools, recreational facilities, churches, and the local American Red Cross chapter in your community. Take a course with your family or a group of friends. You'll help each other learn about water safety and have more fun, too.

Have an Emergency Plan

You should have an emergency plan for responding to water accidents wherever you swim.

If you're using a community pool or supervised beach, look for information about the emergency plan for that location. Follow the lifeguard's instructions if there is an emergency. If there is no emergency plan displayed, get emergency information from your city, county, or state authorities.

It's best to swim at a supervised area, but if you're swimming at your own pool, pond, or any unsupervised area, develop your own emergency plan.

Here are the basic elements of an emergency plan:

- **An emergency signal**—Blow a whistle or horn, or wave a flag to alert swimmers that they should leave the water immediately. At a home pool or pond, the signal will tell other family members and neighbors that there is an emergency and help is needed quickly.

- **Safety equipment for private swimming areas and other areas without lifeguards**—Attach a ring buoy or other safety device to a white or yellow safety post close to the water. A well-stocked first aid kit should also be readily available.

- **Emergency procedures**—Develop and post procedures for what to do in a water emergency. All procedures must be carefully planned. At public facilities, follow the lifeguard's instructions during emergencies. At home pools or ponds, teach your family and friends the procedures. Tell your neighbors about your procedures so they can assist if necessary.

Understand the Emergency Medical Services (EMS) System

An emergency medical services (EMS) system is a community-wide, coordinated means of responding to an accident or a medical emergency. People trained in first aid are the first link in a community's emergency response chain. When you come upon the scene of an accident, and after you have completed an initial (primary) survey, you can activate a professional system that provides advanced care and skilled transfer of the victim to a medical facility. EMS should be activated for life-threatening conditions that require the assistance of trained medical professionals. Situations requiring the activation of EMS include: near-drownings; spinal injuries; cardiac or respiratory emergencies; the presence of severe bleeding; medical conditions or acute illnesses such as severe asthma, repetitive seizures, diabetic emergencies, stroke, or poisoning; and trauma-related accidents resulting in possible fracures or multiple injuries.

Prehospital EMS care provides an arm of the hospital emergency room that extends into the community. EMS teams will respond quickly with the knowledge and the necessary equipment to rescue, stabilize, and transport victims.

You should be aware, however, that not all ambulances are staffed and equipped to provide advanced care to the victim at the scene of an emergency. But in most cases it is better to call for an ambulance to transport the victim, rather than to transport the victim yourself. The victim's condition could worsen on the way to the hospital, and an ambulance is equipped and staffed to deal with conditions that could develop during the transport. In addition, transporting a victim in a private vehicle places tremendous emotional pressure on the driver. This puts all occupants of the vehicle at added risk.

It is important to be familiar with the emergency resources of your community and develop a plan of action before an emergency happens.

Many communities have a 9-1-1 emergency number telephone system to activate the EMS system. By dialing 9-1-1, people in the community can activate an ambulance service, the police department, and the fire department. Some communities have a local number to call for an ambulance; in others, the operator forwards emergency calls. Be sure to know what number to use in your community.

• **Making the call**
Make the call to EMS yourself, or give that responsibility to by-standers. If possible, send two people to make the call, to ensure it is made accurately. Instruct the caller(s) to report back to you and tell you what the dispatcher said.

It is very important to stay on the phone after you have given all of the information listed below in case the EMS dispatcher has any further questions. Make sure that the dispatcher has all the information to get the right help to the scene quickly. Be prepared to tell the dispatcher—
• The location of the emergency (exact address, city or town, nearby intersections or landmarks, name of facility).
• The telephone number of the phone being used.
• The caller's name.
• What happened.
• The number of victims.
• The victims' conditions.
• The help being given.

Preventing Water Accidents

Remember—do not hang up first, because the dispatcher may need more information. For a more detailed description of the EMS system, see the Appendix.

A tear-out form for emergency numbers also appears in the Appendix. Complete all the information on this tear-out form and post it next to your telephone.

Conditions to Look for Before You Swim

	Swimming pools	Ponds, rivers, or lakes	Ocean beaches
Lifeguards	X	X	X
Clean water	X	X	X
Clean, well-maintained beach and deck areas	X	X	X
Nonslip surfaces	X	X	X
Free of electrical equipment or power lines	X	X	X
Emergency communication to get help	X	X	X
Safety equipment	X	X	X
Supervision for children and nonswimmers	X	X	X
Clearly marked water depths	X	X	X
Buoyed lines to separate shallow and deep water	X	X	
Firm and gently sloping bottom		X	X
No sudden drop-offs, large logs, submerged objects		X	X
Well-constructed rafts, piers, docks		X	X
Free of dangerous currents		X	X
Free of dangerous aquatic life		X	X
Signals for wave conditions		X*	X

*For very large lakes

Personal Flotation Devices (PFDs)

You should wear or have available personal flotation devices (PFDs) when you are in, on, or around the water. There are five basic types of PFDs.

- **Type I**
  Life preserver—Designed to turn an unconscious person in the water from a facedown position to a vertical or slightly tipped-back position *(Fig. 1)*.

- **Type II**
  Buoyant vest—Designed to turn an unconscious person in the water from a facedown position to a vertical or slightly tipped-back position. Buoyant vests offer less buoyancy than Type I PFDs *(Fig. 2)*.

- **Type III**
  Special purpose device—Designed to keep a conscious person in a vertical or slightly tipped-back position *(Fig. 3)*. Type III PFDs are more comfortable for active water sports than Types I and II.

- **Type IV**
  Buoyant cushion and ring buoy—Designed to be thrown to a victim in an emergency, but not designed to be worn *(Fig. 4)*. A buoyant cushion can be used as a seat cushion.

Figure 1
Type I: Life Preserver

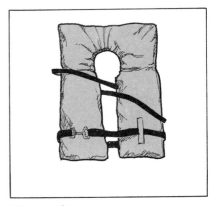

Figure 2
Type II: Buoyant Vest

Figure 3
Type III: Special Purpose Device

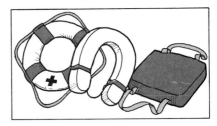

Figure 4
Type IV: Buoyant Cushion and Ring Buoy

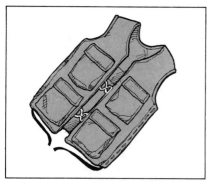

Figure 5
Type V: Restricted-Use

• *Type V*
Restricted-use PFD—A special purpose device approved for special activities, such as commercial white water rafting, where a life preserver device would interfere or when more protection is needed *(Fig. 5)*.

When you choose a PFD—
• Make sure it's approved by the Coast Guard.
• Make sure it's the proper size.
• Practice putting it on in shallow water and swimming with it. When you practice, have a companion with you who can help you if you have difficulty.
• Wear the Coast Guard–approved PFD whenever there's a chance that you could fall or be thrown into the water; for example, when you're boating, tubing or rafting, or walking alongside rapids.

Potential Hazards

Danger is the last thing you want to think about when you're getting ready to enjoy the water. However, you may prevent an accident by taking the time to learn about potential dangers.

It's especially important to remember that the potential hazards change from area to area throughout the country. If you're planning to swim in a new area, check it out first!

Among the potential hazards are—
• Waves
• Currents
• Dams
• Aquatic life
• Objects concealed underwater and varying water depths
• Bad weather conditions
• Panic
• Cramps
• Exhaustion
• Hyperventilation
• Sunburn, heat stroke, heat exhaustion
• Problems affecting personal hygiene
• Inappropriate clothing
• Uncontrolled long hair

Waves

Waves are usually caused by the wind. Large, steep waves breaking close to shore can knock you from your feet and roll you under the surface *(Fig. 6)*. The short, choppy waves of larger lakes can be as strong as ocean swells. Even waves at a wave pool or water park can catch you off guard.

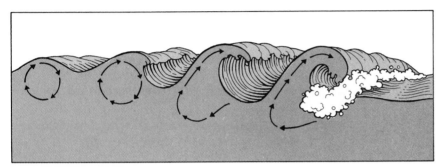

Figure 6
Waves

Swimmers are often surprised by large waves caused by motor boats. A large wave quickly followed by other waves can suddenly push a rubber raft or inner tube away from the swimmer or surprise the swimmer with a sudden splash of water in the face.

Currents

Currents are a danger to swimmers in rivers and open water. Currents can carry you a great distance, often before you realize it. The types of currents to watch out for are river currents, hydraulic currents, and ocean currents. If you're caught in a current, don't try to fight it and don't swim against it. You'll only wear yourself out.

Types of Currents and How to Escape Them

River Current

What it is:
White water, fast-moving water; unpredictable, often changing direction.

How to escape:
Roll over onto your back and go downstream feetfirst *(Fig. 7)*. When you are finally out of the rapids, swim downstream at an angle toward shore *(Fig. 8)*.

Figure 7
Feetfirst Downstream

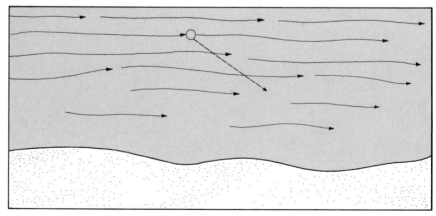

Figure 8
Angle Toward Shore

Hydraulic Current

What it is: Vertical whirlpool created as water flows over an object.

How to escape: Swim to the bottom and swim out with the current before surfacing *(Fig. 9)*.

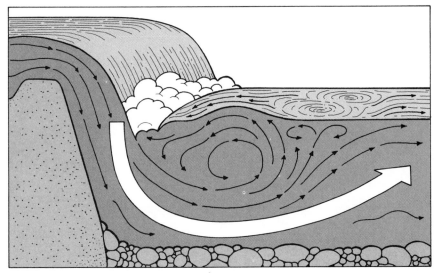

Figure 9
Hydraulic Current

Ocean Currents (three types)

What they are: 1. Drift or side current (littoral) that moves **parallel to the shore,** and carries the swimmer farther down the beach *(Fig. 10)*.

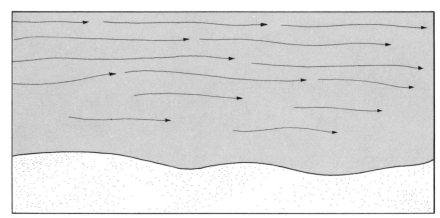

Figure 10
Littoral Current

2. Backwash (undertow) water that moves down the slope of the beach under incoming waves *(Fig. 11)*. Backwash moves **straight out**.

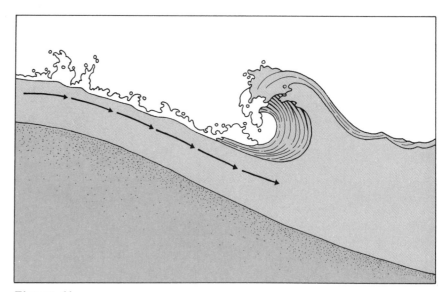

Figure 11
Backwash (Undertow)

3. Rip currents move **straight out** to sea beyond the wave-break areas *(Fig. 12)*. Rip currents can move a swimmer into deep water.

How to escape: If an ocean current carries you parallel to shore, swim toward the shore while the current carries you in its direction of flow. (You'll eventually get to shore although you may be some distance from where you entered the water.) If an ocean current carries you straight out, swim away from it by moving parallel to the shore. When you're free of it, turn to the shore *(Fig. 13)*.

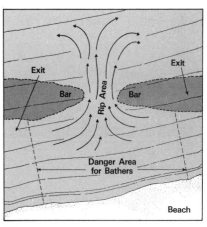

Figure 12
Rip Current

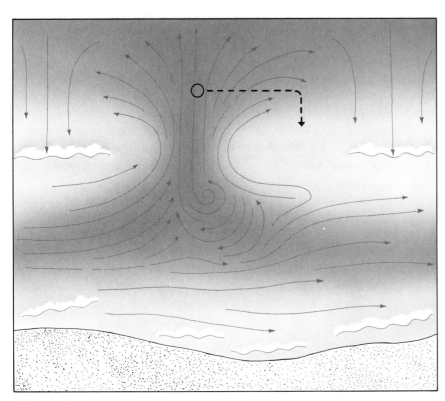

Figure 13
Rip Current Escape

Preventing Water Accidents

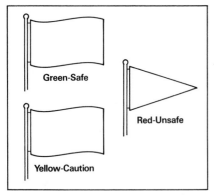

Figure 14
Warning Flags for Swimming

When you arrive at the beach, check to see if the lifeguard has raised a warning flag or a flag that means water conditions are safe for swimming *(Fig. 14)*.

Warning Flags for Waves and Currents

Green flag—safe, facility open for swimming
Red flag—unsafe, facility closed
Yellow flag—caution, limited swimming because of currents or
other conditions

If you're going canoeing, boating, or rafting in moving water, you must be properly trained; you must have the right equipment; and you should be supervised by an expert guide who knows the waterway. Be careful to keep your footing when you're walking alongside or in rapids. Always wear a Coast Guard–approved PFD.

Dams

Dams at large lakes or ponds and low-head dams on rivers can cause hazards for swimmers. When floodgates open, the water level can rise quickly below the dam, often creating a wall of water.

If there are any gates open at a hydroelectric power dam, the current can pull swimmers and even boaters in the lake into dangerous areas of the dam. The area just below a dam may collect a hazardous build-up of debris or silt.

A low-head dam—a manufactured structure at or just below the surface of a river—can be very dangerous. If you're swimming, boating, or rafting, you should be aware of and avoid low-head dams. When water flows over a low-head dam, a dangerous hydraulic current is often created. Even canoes and other types of boats have been caught in hydraulic currents. Check the river out before you get in or on the water. Swimming or boating near a dam is dangerous.

Quick review: Make sure you know what the water conditions are and which ones are safe or dangerous for swimming. Wear a Coast Guard–approved PFD if you're around moving water or in a boat.

Aquatic Life

Aquatic life, which includes plants and animals, varies with location. Ocean beaches, rivers, lakes, and ponds across the country all have different kinds of aquatic life. Check with local authorities, such as fish and wildlife officers, about the types of potentially dangerous plants and animals to watch out for when you go swimming.

Weeds, grass, and kelp grow in most natural water environments. It's best not to swim in areas of heavy growth, because you could easily become entangled. If you find yourself entangled in underwater plants, remember that the more you thrash about, the more

14

tightly they wrap around you. You should slowly and gently withdraw from them.

If you're in a current, move slowly in its direction. The current will help untangle the plants. If you see or feel a patch of plants on the surface, don't try to swim through them. Avoid them if you can.

Aquatic animals generally do not pose a threat to swimmers *(Figs. 15–18)*. At ocean areas, you may find stinging animals, such as jellyfish or Portuguese man-of-war. Animal stings can cause discomfort, pain, and in some extreme cases, even illness or death.

In fresh water you might see snakes or leeches, but snakes normally avoid people, and leeches are more of a nuisance than a danger.

If you come upon an animal, do not touch it but move away slowly. If the animal poses a danger to other swimmers, note its exact location and tell the lifeguard or other authority. Above all, leave it alone.

Know where you can get medical attention if you or anyone in your group is stung or bitten by an aquatic animal. Find out about the various types of aquatic life in your area or any area you are going to swim in.

Quick review: *Make sure you know about the various forms of aquatic life where you're swimming. Make sure you can get medical attention quickly if you need it.*

Objects Concealed Underwater and Varying Water Depths

Serious injury can occur if you jump, slide, or dive into water and strike either the bottom or an object concealed beneath the surface, such as a tree stump, a concrete slab, or an old support beam for a dock. Always check out an area carefully before you swim or dive. When you go in the first time, enter the water slowly and go in feetfirst.

Moving water, wind, and man-made structures often change the shape and depth of the bottom. Even if you go to the same swimming area each year, always check it out first!

Bad Weather Conditions

Bad weather can be hazardous to swimmers. You shouldn't swim when there's lightning, thunderstorms, heavy rain or hail, tornadoes, fog, or high winds. You shouldn't be in or on a river when flooding has occurred or is anticipated, and you should avoid trying out the big waves when a hurricane is approaching.

If a storm is approaching, leave the water when you hear the first sound of thunder. Go into a large building or other enclosed shelter. Stay away from open areas, heights, or anything metal. If there is no shelter, crouch on the ground but don't go under a tree or utility pole.

Figure 15
Aquatic Animals: Jellyfish and Portuguese Man-of-War

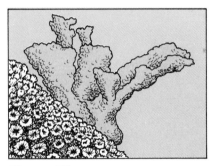

Figure 16
Aquatic Animals: Stinging Coral

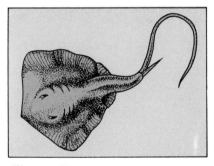

Figure 17
Aquatic Animals: Sting Ray

Figure 18
Aquatic Animals: Cone

Estimating the distance to the thunderstorm is relatively easy. When you see lightning, begin counting seconds—saying "one thousand" before each count will take up a second. Count until you hear the thunder. Divide the number of seconds between the lightning and the thunder by five to estimate the distance to the storm in miles. Divide the number of seconds by three to obtain the distance in kilometers. For example:

1. You see lightning.
2. Begin counting — one thousand one, one thousand two, one thousand three, and so on.
3. You hear thunder.
4. Stop counting. Let's assume you counted six seconds.
5. Divide by five to determine the distance in miles. The storm is approximately 1.2 miles away. (To find the distance in kilometers, divide by three. The storm is approximately two kilometers away.)

Quick review: Check for water depth, check for underwater obstacles, check for other area hazards before you swim. Leave the water at the first sign of threatening weather.

Panic

Panic is a sudden and overwhelming terror that can make you unable to help yourself or someone else, and it occurs in most water accidents. Many hazards, such as getting caught in weeds or suffering cramps, can produce the serious added effect of panic.

Even the skilled and experienced swimmer can panic. But the more skilled you are and the more you know about water safety, the more effective you will be in an emergency. Having a personal emergency plan is the best way to prevent panic and accidents.

If you must respond to a dangerous situation, you need to act quickly. If you act rashly, you could make the emergency worse. If you suddenly find yourself in trouble, remember that you may have more time than you realize to think about what you should do.

If you're trying to help someone who's struggling in the water, be certain not to put yourself in danger. Look around for a way to extend your reach to the victim, rather than leaping into the water yourself. (See the section How to Help Others in an Emergency, page 43, for more information.)

You can help a panicky victim by speaking calmly and explaining that assistance is on the way. You can also try to instruct the victim on how to get out of danger or how to make it easier for you to help.

Any time you are near water, it's a good idea to think ahead and plan what to do if something should go wrong. Be prepared!

Cramps

Cramps occur when one of your muscles, usually in your arm, foot, or calf, involuntarily contracts into a knot. Cramps can be caused by fatigue, cold, or overexertion, and they often occur early in the swimming season when many people are not yet in shape. To prevent cramps, be moderate in your recreation activities. When you get a cramp, try to relax the affected muscle by changing its position and kneading or massaging it with your hands.

If you're in the water and get a cramp, try not to become alarmed. Often, simply changing your swimming stroke will relieve the cramp. If that doesn't work, change the position of the muscle while you massage it. If you get a foot or leg cramp while you're in deep water, take a deep breath, roll facedown, extend your leg, flex your foot, and massage the cramp *(Fig. 19)*.

Occasionally, swimmers suffer abdominal cramps. These, too, are caused by fatigue, cold, or overexertion. They are **not** caused by swimming too soon after eating, as commonly thought. Severe abdominal cramps are rare.

In mild cases of abdominal cramps, relax and try to maintain your position in the water while the cramp passes. If someone in your group suffers a severe cramp, get the person to safety as quickly as possible.

Exhaustion

Exhaustion simply means that you no longer have the energy to make progress through the water or to float. Exhaustion can occur—

- As a reaction to cold water.
- As a result of lying in the sun too long.
- If you're very tired when you enter the water.
- If you swim too long and too hard.

Early swimming-season fatigue is a serious problem, especially for younger swimmers who do too much before they're really in shape.

Prevent exhaustion by resting frequently while you're enjoying the water. Watch all the members of your swimming party for the signs that someone is becoming chilled—shivering, cold and clammy skin, or a bluish tinge to the lips.

In particular, look out for the younger swimmers, who may become chilled or exhausted before they realize they're in danger.

Hyperventilation

Hyperventilation is repeated deep breathing. Some swimmers try to increase their breath-holding time for underwater swimming by hyperventilating or "blowing off" carbon dioxide.

This practice is dangerous because the level of carbon dioxide in your blood is what signals your body to take each breath. If you hyperventilate and then swim underwater, you could actually pass out before your body knows it's time to breathe. By the time

Case History

It is important to stay calm in an emergency.

It was early in the season and a college student was working at a summer camp. She was a good swimmer and knew water safety practices. She and some other counselors decided to go for a swim one afternoon. While the student was performing the breaststroke kick, her foot became severely cramped.

Even though she was in great pain, she calmly asked her companions for help. The others carefully assisted her to the dock, using a nearby kickboard for extra support.

If the student had panicked, her rescue would have been much more difficult for the others—and she might have drowned.

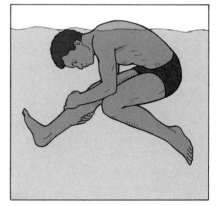

Figure 19
Leg Cramp Release

17

your companions notice you've been under too long, it could easily be too late. If you enjoy underwater swimming, learn how to improve your skills with a certified Red Cross instructor. *Don't hyperventilate!*

Sunburn, Heat Stroke, Heat Exhaustion

These problems often occur when swimmers play too long and hard or stay too long in the sun. Some people don't realize how the sun can affect them.

Because sunlight reflects off shiny surfaces such as bodies of water, being around water can increase your exposure. Sunburn can occur on overcast days as well as on sunny days.

Increase your activities gradually as you get in better shape. When you're in the sun, wear a sunscreen lotion, which blocks some sun rays, or a sunblock lotion, which provides maximum protection. Wear sunglasses and a hat, and drink plenty of nonalcoholic liquids.

The following information tells how to recognize heat exhaustion and heat stroke, and what to do for victims:

	Heat Exhaustion	Heat Stroke
What to look for:	Cool, pale, and moist skin; heavy sweating; headache; nausea; dizziness; and vomiting. Body temperature will be nearly normal.	Hot, red skin; shock or unconsciousness; and very high body temperature—sometimes as high as 105 °F. Skin will feel dry (unless the victim was sweating from heavy work or exercise, or if the victim had just been in the water).

	Heat Exhaustion	Heat Stroke
What to do:	Treat heat exhaustion as an emergency. Call for emergency medical assistance. Have the victim lie in the coolest place available. Place the victim on the back with the feet raised. Rub the victim's body with a cool, wet cloth. Give the victim one-half glassful of water to drink every 15 minutes, if he or she is fully conscious and can tolerate it. These steps should bring improvement within a half hour. Medical attention may be necessary.	Treat heat stroke as a life-threatening emergency. Call for emergency medical assistance immediately. Cool the victim by any available means. Place the victim in a cool bath, pour cool water over the body, or wrap wet sheets around the body and fan it. Care for shock. Give nothing by mouth.

Quick review: Practice moderation when you swim. Don't swim or play too hard for too long. Avoid long periods in cool water or out in the sun. Don't overtax your swimming skills.

Problems of Personal Hygiene

These problems occur in community swimming pools. Although pool chemicals help keep the water clean and safe for swimming, they can't make the water completely sterile. Use only those community pools where personal hygiene regulations are strictly enforced (for example, soap showers are required before swimming). Color and clarity of water are good indicators of the water condition.

Swimming in Inappropriate Clothing

Inappropriate clothing can be hazardous in the water. Clothing such as sweatshirts or long pants can absorb a great deal of water and become extremely heavy. Make sure that what you wear for swimming won't become a burden to you in the water.

Uncontrolled Long Hair

Long hair can be a hazard to swimmers. It can become entangled in underwater objects, get in your eyes or mouth, or interfere with breathing. Always tie long hair back or wear a bathing cap.

Quick review: Dress correctly for water recreation. Use only those community pools that enforce personal hygiene rules—and obey them yourself.

Safety Tips for Swimming

Here are basic tips to follow whenever and wherever you swim (pools in motels, hotels, or apartment complexes; community pools; home pools; lakes; ponds; rivers; or oceans):

- Always swim with companions. Swim only in areas well supervised by lifeguards.
- Never drink alcohol or use drugs when you're swimming or boating.
- Always check the water depth. Walk in from shore or ease in from the dock or the edge of the pool.
- Don't swim if you can't see the bottom of the pool in the deep end, or if the water is cloudy.
- Stay close enough to the shore or pool's edge so you can get to safety by yourself.
- Know the limits of your own swimming abilities. If you're a good swimmer, don't tempt nonswimmers or beginner swimmers to try to keep up with you. Instead, encourage them to stay at a safe depth.
- Watch out for the "dangerous too's"—too tired, too cold, too far from safety, too much sun, too much hard playing.
- Stay out of the water when you're overheated or overtired.
- Keep an eye on younger swimmers at all times.
- Follow the lifeguards' instructions and respect their judgment. Never fake an emergency. Obey all swimming rules.
- Learn the proper way to dive in the water safely. Follow the guidelines in this book for safe diving.
- Don't chew gum or eat while you swim. It is dangerous and you could easily choke.
- Wear goggles for surface swimming only, not for underwater swimming.

When You're at the Beach
- Locate the nearest lifeguard stand.
- Know the surf conditions before you enter the water. Check to see if a warning flag is flying.
- Swim well away from piers, pilings, and diving platforms.
- Look out for potentially dangerous aquatic life.
- Save enough energy to swim back to shore safely.
- Remember that if you are caught in a current, you can make it back to shore by swimming gradually away from the current. Don't try to swim against it.

When You Go to Community Pools
- Obey all pool rules.
- Remember that pushing, shoving, and running around the pool can be dangerous.
- Follow the lifeguard's directions carefully in an actual emergency or a drill.

- Check water depth. The first time you enter the water, ease in from the side of the pool.
- Go down water slides in a sitting position with your feet first.
- Swim a safe distance away from diving boards.
- Use diving boards properly.

When You Go to a Wave Pool or Water Park
- Be sure all areas are well supervised by lifeguards before you enter the water.
- Follow all rules and directions.
- Watch out for floating objects in wave pools when the wave machine is on. Before you enter the water, be sure you know the water depth. There will usually be a signal right before the waves begin.
- Remember, when you slide down a flume, or water chute, you'll be going down fast, so position yourself carefully before you start down.
- Go down slides in a sitting position with your feet first.
- Don't let anyone pressure you into trying a dangerous stunt on a slide or flume.

When You Swim in Lakes, Ponds, Rivers, or Creeks
- Swim only in areas supervised by lifeguards. Find out where and how to get emergency assistance.
- Avoid swimming near dams, diving platforms, or boat ramps.
- Find out about the local aquatic life.
- Check water depth. The first time you enter the water, walk in carefully.
- Find out about dams, locks, or other facilities that might affect the water level.
- Look for underwater obstacles and dangerous debris, such as bottles or cans.
- Be aware of changing river currents. Avoid rivers and creeks when there is any chance of flooding.

When You Own the Pond
- Enroll in a water safety course to learn more about potential dangers and the prevention of accidents in, on, and around the water.
- Have the health department check and approve the water for swimming.
- Mark off safe swimming areas with buoyed lines *(Fig. 20)*. Mark any underwater obstacles or other danger spots with secured, floating markers, such as plastic jugs or buoys.
- Set up a safety post with ring buoys and other safety equipment. (See the section How to Help Others in an Emergency, page 43, for more information on safety equipment.)

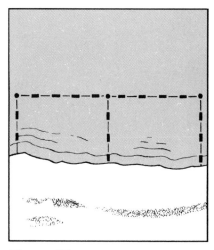

Figure 20
Buoyed Line in Lake

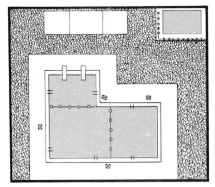

Figure 21
Buoyed Lines in Pool

- Draw up an emergency plan, and make sure all swimmers know about it. Post the plan at the pond. Emergency telephone numbers and directions to the pond should be posted by the nearest telephone.
- Never permit anyone to swim alone in your pond.

When You Own the Pool

- Enroll in a water safety course to learn as much as you can about pool safety and the causes and prevention of swimming pool accidents.
- Find out about your state and community regulations regarding such matters as pool fencing, filtration, and pool chemicals.
- Use buoyed lines to mark where water depth changes from shallow to deep water *(Figs. 21 and 22)*.

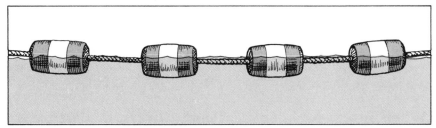

Figure 22
Buoyed Line

- Set up a safety post with ring buoys or other safety equipment. (See the section How to Help Others in an Emergency, page 43, for more information on safety equipment.)
- Post a set of rules for your pool and enforce them without exception. For example, don't allow bottles or glass in the pool area; don't allow running or pushing; don't allow diving in the shallow water.
- Post an emergency plan where everyone will see it. Post emergency phone numbers by the nearest telephone. Also post the directions to your address so that anyone can read them to an emergency dispatcher.
- Never permit anyone to swim alone in your pool.
- Properly fence and secure your pool area to prevent people from entering without your knowledge and to protect children who may be tempted by the water.
- Store pool chemicals—chlorine, soda ash, muriatic acid, test kits—in child-proof containers and out of children's reach. Clearly label the chemicals. Follow the directions and safety instructions from the chemical manufacturers.

Safety Tips for Other Recreational Water Activities

Aquatic recreation is a leading pastime activity in this country. We often participate in other aquatic recreation that may not include swimming. Boating, fishing, and hunting are all examples. This section provides some basic tips to follow for other aquatic activities.

Infant and Preschool Swimming

Even though a child may demonstrate some swimming ability, no child should ever be considered totally safe around the water. Children must be carefully supervised by an adult at all times.

The American Red Cross Infant and Preschool Aquatic Program offers a water adjustment and swimming readiness progression for infants (6 months to 18 months), toddlers (18 months to 36 months), and preschoolers (3 through 5 years) and their parents.

Any time you take a child swimming, remember that infants and young children are very susceptible to hypothermia, even at relatively warm temperatures. Water temperatures should be a minimum of 82°F. Air temperature should be three degrees higher than the water temperature. You should limit the child's swimming time to 30 minutes or less in the water. If the child shivers or has blue lips or blue fingernails, take the child out of the water immediately. Remember: Watch children in, on, or near the water at all times, and carefully supervise their water play.

Ice Skating and Ice Fishing

Before you go onto the ice, make sure the ice surface is safe. Always take a safety device with you. (See the section Ice Safety, page 58.)

Hunting and Fishing

Anytime you are near water, you should dress appropriately for the weather, wear a Coast Guard–approved PFD, and have some type of reaching device nearby. If you're walking alongside water, pay attention to your footing. If you're using a small boat, guard against losing your balance. Remember that if you drink alcohol you are more likely to have an accident. (See sections Boating Safety, page 68; Sudden Immersion, page 36; and Exposure to Cold Water, page 58.)

Surfing, Windsurfing, and Bodysurfing

Before you take part in these activities, take lessons from a qualified instructor to learn how to surf. Be sure water and weather conditions are safe. Remember that surfing moves you through the water very quickly. Watch out for your board—if it hits you, you could be injured seriously or even knocked unconscious. Wear a Coast Guard–approved PFD.

Snorkeling and Scuba Diving

Check with a qualified instructor before you obtain diving equipment or explore underwater. Enroll in a certified course whose focus is on snorkeling and scuba diving safety. (More information is available in the *American Red Cross Emergency Water Safety* textbook.)

Water Skiing

Check the water for hidden stumps or other obstacles that might cause a skier to fall. The skier should wear a Coast Guard–approved PFD. Another person, other than the operator of the boat, should watch the skier at all times. Boat operators need to be competent and drive safely. Make sure that the boat and skiing equipment are in good repair. Check that all safety equipment is on the boat.

Take your skiing seriously and don't clown around. Remember that being towed by a fast-moving boat puts you in a potentially dangerous situation.

Tubing and Rafting

Wear a Coast Guard–approved PFD when you're tubing or rafting. There's always a possibility that your inner tube or raft could be punctured and that you could find yourself in deep water or rapids. If you're rafting with tour guides, make sure that they are fully qualified.

Boating, Canoeing, and Sailing

Before you go out on the water, learn how to maneuver small crafts by taking lessons from a qualified Red Cross instructor.

Inspect the craft, the equipment, and the PFDs. Each occupant should wear a Coast Guard–approved PFD. Be sure to carry appropriate safety equipment.

Check the weather before you start boating, and return to shore if threatening weather develops while you're boating. Check with the local authorities about water levels, dams, or other facilities. (See the section Boating Safety, page 68.)

Always notify somebody about your trip: where and when you are going and when you plan to return. This is often called a "float plan."

Water Polo and Other Water Sports

Before you participate in water sports, you should be in good physical condition. Learn the rules of the game and abide by them.

Avoid cuts and punctures. Keep your fingernails and toenails short to avoid cutting others. Don't wear jewelry.

Summer Camp

Before choosing a summer camp, find out about the condition of the camp's waterfront and how the staff will supervise water activities.

The American Camping Association's waterfront standard requires that a waterfront supervisor be well qualified and certified in water safety by the American Red Cross, YMCA, or Boy Scouts of America. All other waterfront staff should be well trained and certified.

The waterfront area should be free of hazards and well marked. There should be lifeguards as well as two or three systems for checking on swimmers, such as the following:

- **Buddy system**—Each swimmer pairs off with a buddy, and they stay alert to each other's activities at all times.

- **Check board system**—Each swimmer entering the water turns over a name tag on a check board and then turns the tag again after leaving the water.

- **Colored caps**—Each swimmer wears a cap whose color indicates swimming ability. The waterfront staff can easily spot when swimmers are outside of the proper swimming area or participating in activities beyond their abilities.

- **Roll call**—Swimmers are checked in and out of the water by calling a roll.

Also ask the camp about the other types of waterfront activities and the qualifications of staff responsible for swimming, canoeing, sailing, diving, scuba diving, or water skiing.

Spas and Hot Tubs

People can drown at spas and in hot tubs, so supervision is imperative. Also, make sure the facility is regularly maintained for proper sanitation and safety.

According to the National Spa and Pool Institute, the maximum safe water temperature is 104 °F. Don't soak for more than 15 minutes at one sitting. Soaking too long at too high a water temperature can raise your body temperature over safe limits.

Spas and hot tubs should be securely covered to prevent anyone from falling in accidently. The cover should be removed completely before use, so that the people soaking in the spa or hot tub are clearly visible.

If you have long hair, tie it back or wear a bathing cap to prevent your hair from getting pulled into the the drainage opening.

People with certain illnesses, diseases, or medical conditions, and people taking certain types of medications should not use a spa or hot tub without their physician's approval. If you have any doubts about whether you should use a hot tub, check with your physician or health care provider.

Never use a spa or hot tub if you are under the influence of alcohol or drugs.

Case History

Before you dive, you must check the depth of the water and the condition of the bottom of the body of water. If you dive without checking, you risk a bad accident, as in the following example:

A group of high school students went to a lake for a picnic. Some of the boys began jumping off a bridge into the water, and they dared others to follow.

One young man finally accepted the dares of his companions and leaped over the railing. He landed in three feet of water where the bottom of the lake had been reinforced with concrete. He broke an arm and a leg but could easily have been paralyzed or killed.

If the young man had checked, he would have discovered that the water was too shallow for diving or jumping and that there was concrete on the bottom. In any case, he should have ignored the dares of his companions to take part in such dangerous activity.

Diving Safety

Improper diving causes the greatest number of serious spinal cord injuries of all sports, according to *Spinal Cord Injury: The Facts and Figures,* A Spinal Cord Injury Data Base at the University of Alabama in Birmingham.

You can be seriously injured by diving into shallow water, diving improperly, diving into unknown water, going down water slides headfirst, falling off a diving board, or diving from racing blocks without proper training. You can be badly hurt by hitting the bottom or striking an underwater object.

A very large percentage of diving-related spinal cord injuries result in complete quadriplegia—total paralysis from the neck down.

Tips for Safe Diving

- Learn how to dive properly from a qualified Red Cross instructor. The approach on the diving board, the takeoff, the entry into the water—each stage of diving is important to safety. The "self-taught" diver is clearly more likely to have an accident. Learn how to do it right!
- Follow all safety rules.
- Do not wear earplugs, which can cause additional dangerous pressure on your ears as you dive.
- Do not wear goggles except under the supervision of a qualified coach in competitive swimming.
- Obey "No Diving" signs. They are there for your safety.
- Check for adequate water depth. When you first enter the water, ease in or walk in, don't jump or dive. Never dive in shallow water or above-ground pools. Even at the edge of a pool or dock, diving into water less than nine feet deep is potentially dangerous. There is always a possibility of injury if you go straight down in the water and strike the bottom. To dive off a low diving board, the water depth should be a minimum of 10 feet. In smaller pools, that depth might not be enough. The higher the board, the deeper the water should be.
- Before you dive, check for objects hidden beneath the surface of the water, such as logs or pilings.
- Check the shape of the pool bottom to be sure the water is deep enough where you will actually be entering and submerging.
- Make sure all surfaces—diving boards, decks, and other areas for walking—are nonslip.
- Remember that the presence of a diving board doesn't necessarily mean that diving is safe. Pools at homes, motels, and hotels often do not have an area deep enough for safe diving.
- Allow only one person on the diving board at a time.
- Dive only from the end of the board, not from the side.
- Remember that bouncing repeatedly on the diving board can make you lose your footing.

- Plan your dive so you'll be ready to steer up toward the surface immediately after you enter the water.
- Swim away from the diving board after you dive.
- Don't allow anyone in your group to pressure or dare anyone else into diving dangerously.
- Go down slides in a sitting position with your feet first. Only use slides that are located in the deep end of the pool.
- Remember that diving from starting blocks can be dangerous. Starting blocks should be used only by trained competitive swimmers under the supervision of a qualified coach.

Tips for Diving at the Beach or in the Surf
- Find out where the shallow and deep areas of the water are located. Remember, the ocean floor is constantly shifting.
- Don't jump or dive into water from a pier or rock jetty.
- Remember, running from the beach into water and then diving headfirst into the waves is dangerous.
- If you're bodysurfing, always keep your arms out in front of you to protect your head and neck.

Planning Your Dive
There are three types of dives: long shallow, racing, and deep. When you dive, you should prepare to steer up to the surface once you've entered the water.
- When you're ready to dive, extend your arms over your head with your elbows locked. Keep your arms extended and your hands together. Your upper arms should be close against your ears, and your hands should be flat. This position will give you some protection if you strike anything underwater, and you'll be ready to steer up.
- After you've entered the water, steer up by pointing your fingers toward the surface, arching your back, and looking up to the surface of the water.

Guidelines for Deep Diving Safety

Diving location	Safety standards
From the edge of a pool or the edge of a low dock	Minimum water depth of 9 feet. Taller or heavier divers who use a vertical entry may require deeper water.
From a recreational springboard or jumpboard	If the board is 30 inches above the water, the water depth should be 9 feet. If the board is one meter (39½ inches) above the water, the water depth should be 10 feet.*
From competitive boards 3 meters above the water	Minimum water depth of 13 feet. 13-foot depth should extend 20 feet forward from dive entry point and 12 feet on either side of the board.

*Minimum Standards for Public Swimming Pools, April 1, 1977 (1/88 printing), National Spa and Pool Institute.

Recommendations for Diving Safety

Diving location	Safety recommendations
From boards or platforms 3 meters or higher	Should be used only by trained divers.
From slides at a pool	No headfirst sliding. Water slides should be located so that entry will be into water at least 9 feet deep.
From slides at water parks or large flumes	Should be used **only** according to park directions and rules and **only** if the swimmer is certain that conditions are safe.
From starting blocks	Should **not** be used by recreational swimmers. Should be installed at the deep end of the pool. Should be used only by trained competitive swimmers under supervision of a qualified coach.

These guidelines and recommendations for safe diving are from various organizations concerned with swimming and diving. For further information, contact the National Collegiate Athletic Association, International Swim and Diving Federation (FINA), or United States Diving. Addresses appear in the Appendixes.

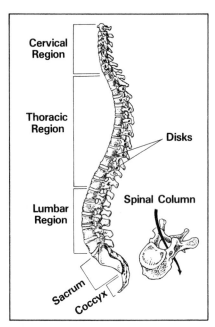

Figure 23
Anatomy of the Spine

Spinal Injury

Most spinal injuries that occur at aquatic facilities are the result of diving in shallow water. Other causes of spinal injury may be jumping, falling, or being pushed against a solid object. Improper use of a water slide may also cause spinal injuries. At many facilities, the slide is positioned into water less than five feet deep. Some swimmers slide down headfirst on their stomachs. The injury can occur when the victim's head hits the bottom of the pool or some other object, such as another swimmer.

Information in this section will help you to recognize a victim with a suspected spinal injury and show you how to assist the victim.

Anatomy and Function of the Spine

You must have a basic understanding of the anatomy and function of the spine in order to make an evaluation of a victim with a suspected back or neck injury.

The spine is a strong, flexible column of small bones (vertebrae) that supports the head and the trunk of your body. The spinal column provides protection to the spinal cord *(Fig. 23)*. Vertebrae are separated from each other by cushions of cartilage called intervertebral disks. This cartilage acts as a shock absorber when a person is walking, running, or jumping.

The spine is divided into five regions: the cervical or neck region, the thoracic or midback region, the lumbar or lower back region, the sacrum, and the coccyx.

Spinal injuries are serious. Diving in shallow or unknown water can cause injuries, paralysis, or death.

Signs and Symptoms

Whether the victim is conscious or unconscious, he or she may display one or more of the following symptoms:
- Pain at the site of a fracture
- Loss of movement in extremities or below the fracture site
- Tingling or loss of feeling in the extremities
- Disorientation
- Neck or back deformity
- Visible bruising over an area of the spinal column
- Impaired breathing
- Head injury
- Fluid/blood in ears

Assessing Spinal Injuries

In trying to determine whether the spinal cord has been injured, you must take into consideration the cause of injury. The following is a general list of situations that may indicate a spinal cord injury:

- Any fall from a height greater than the victim's height
- Any person found unconscious for unknown reasons
- Any significant head trauma
- All diving accidents

Procedures for Assisting the Victim
- Activate the emergency medical services (EMS) system.
- Ease into the water.

If the victim is faceup, use the hip and shoulder support technique.
- Submerge your body to chest depth in the water. Face the victim's side.
- Slide one arm under the victim's shoulders. Slide your other arm under the victim's hip bones and support the victim *(Fig. 24)*.

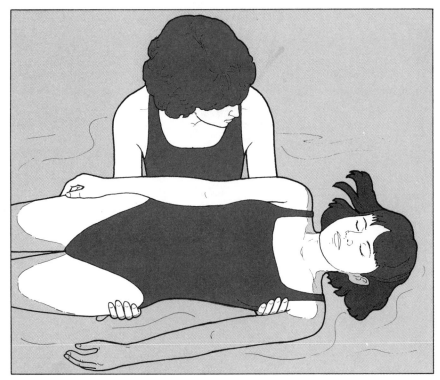

Figure 24
Hip and Shoulder Support

- *Don't lift the victim.* Keep the victim in a horizontal position and offer reassurance.
- Support the victim using the hip and shoulder support until help arrives.

If the victim is facedown, use the head splint support technique.

- Stand facing the victim's side.
- Gently float the victim's arms up alongside the head, parallel to the surface. Do this by grasping the victim's arms midway between the shoulder and elbow *(Fig. 25)*. With your right hand, grasp the victim's right arm. With your left hand, grasp the victim's left arm. Position the arms so they are extended against the victim's head.

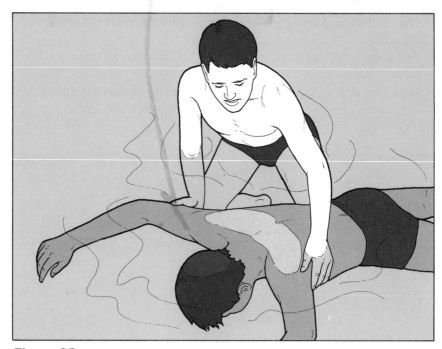

Figure 25
Head Splint: Grasp the Victim's Arms

- When the victim's arms are extended over the head and body, apply pressure to the arms to splint the head *(Fig. 26)*. This is called in-line stabilization. Generally, your hands will be approximately at the victim's ears.

Figure 26
Head Splint: Provide In-Line Stabilization

- Lower your body to chest depth in the water and start to move the victim slowly forward, gliding the victim's body to the surface. This reduces body twist when the turn is made *(Fig. 27)*.

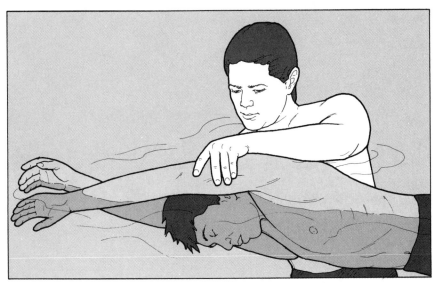

Figure 27
Head Splint: Glide and Rotate Victim Faceup

• Once the victim is horizontal in the water, continue moving and rotate the victim toward you by pushing the arm closer to you under the water, while pulling the victim's other arm across the surface to turn the victim faceup *(Fig. 28)*. As you do this, lower your shoulders in the water.

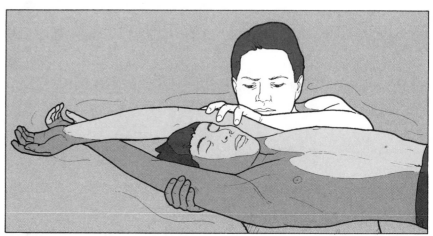

Figure 28
Head Splint: Rotate Victim Faceup

• Rest the victim's head in the crook of your arm, but not on your arm *(Fig. 29)*.

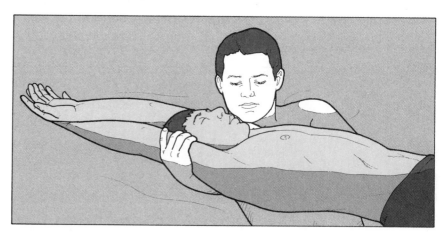

Figure 29
Head Splint: Rest Victim's Head

Emergency Response

Case History

You must be careful around water even if you don't intend to go into it. A water accident and sudden immersion could happen anytime.

A church group was enjoying a picnic at a lake, and a teenager agreed to take 12 children for a boat ride. The teenager had no water recreation or safety training. No one asked whether any of the children could swim. The group went out in an old wooden boat with no personal flotation devices (PFDs).

About 15 yards from shore, the boat began to take on water and sink. One of the children was able to stay near the surface of the water. He was assisted by an elderly fisherman in another boat nearby who heard shouts for help, paddled over, and reached out with a fishing pole.

As the families stood helplessly on shore, the teenager and 11 of the children drowned.

The boat should have been checked carefully before the group went out. All those aboard should have been wearing personal floation devices, and a person trained in water safety should have been on the boat.

Sudden Immersion

In recent years, well over half of drowning victims have been doing something other than swimming or playing in the water. People fishing or hunting around ponds or streams, industrial workers at sites near or above water, or people taking boat rides can often find themselves suddenly in the water.

Water doesn't have to be very deep to be a danger. People have drowned in wells, cisterns, and even standing rainwater. Children have been victims of shallow water drownings around the house, even in the bathtub.

Falling into cold water, and especially having to float in cold water for a long time, can be particularly dangerous. Many hunting and fishing enthusiasts who appeared at first to have drowned, actually died from exposure to cold water.

The most important safety precaution you can take is to remember that water can be hazardous even if you don't intend to go into it.

Safety Precautions to Take When You're Around Water
- Be aware of the possible dangers. Suggest that your companions follow safety precautions, and set a good example yourself.
- Watch children at all times.
- Wear a Coast Guard–approved personal flotation device (PFD), or at least keep PFDs on hand to throw to someone who has fallen into the water.
- Stay with at least one other person around water, just as you would when swimming with a buddy.

Additional Precautions for Industrial Workers
- Learn to swim.
- Take additional courses in water safety and learn how to help yourself or a co-worker in an emergency.
- Remember that you may be required to wear a Coast Guard–approved PFD when you're working at a site near water. Wear nonslip rubber shoes or boots.
- Wear other protection gear as recommended by your industry, such as a flotation jacket or suit.

Quick review: Remember that water can be dangerous even if you don't intend to go in. Take precautions against accidental falls and keep a constant eye on children.

How to Help Yourself in an Emergency

In the following pages, you'll find information on how to help yourself if you fall into water accidentally. To practice some of the techniques, you will need to put your head or face in the water. Note that you should put your head or face in the water only if the water is warm. Body warmth tends to escape quickly through your head and face. Putting your head or face in cold water speeds up this loss of warmth and increases your risk of immersion hypothermia, or cold water exposure.

Water doesn't necessarily have to feel cold to be dangerously cold. If the water even feels cool, don't put your head or face in unless facedown swimming or floating is your last resort for saving your life. (See section Exposure to Cold Water, page 58.)

Swimming Fully Clothed

There are some advantages to keeping your clothes on if you fall into the water. Many types of clothing will actually help you float and will help protect you from cold water.

If your shoes are light enough for you to swim comfortably, leave them on. If they're too heavy, remove them.

Use a swimming stroke that keeps the arms in the water, such as the breaststroke, sidestroke, elementary backstroke, or survival floating travel stroke. Whichever stroke you choose, swim in a way that is most comfortable for you. A perfect technique is not important to sustain yourself.

Treading water will keep you in an upright position while you signal for help or wait for rescue. You may need to tread water while you prepare to use your clothing for flotation. To tread water, remain in a vertical position, submerged to your chin. Use a sculling motion with your hands and use a kick that you can do effectively and comfortably.

Using Your Shirt or Jacket for Flotation

With air trapped in the shoulders of your shirt, you may be able to paddle toward safety. If you need one hand to hold your shirt closed, paddle with the other. There are two ways to use your shirt or jacket for flotation:

- Tuck your shirt in or tie the shirttail ends together. Button or fasten the top button of the shirt up to the neck. Unbutton the second or third button, take a deep breath, bend your head forward, pull the shirt up to your face, and blow into the shirt *(Fig. 30)*. The front of the shirt must be underwater. The air will rise and form a bubble in the shoulders of the shirt, which will help you float.

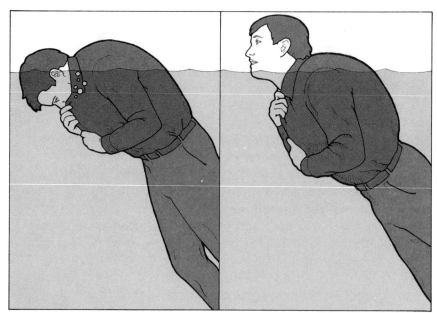

Figure 30
Exhale Into Shirt

- Inflate your shirt by splashing air into it *(Fig. 31)*. Float on your back and hold the front of the shirttail with one hand, keeping it just under the surface of the water. Strike the water with your free hand palm down from above the surface of the water to a point below the shirttail. The air, carried down from the surface, will bubble into the shirt.

Figure 31
Splash Air Into Jacket

Quick review: Clothing can actually help you in a water emergency. Learn how to use clothing to help you float.

Bobbing

You should learn and practice bobbing. Even nonswimmers can quickly learn to bob in shallow water. Practicing both breath control and bobbing will make you more comfortable and better able to help yourself if you fall into the water. When you practice, make sure you have a companion present who can help you if you have difficulty.

Remember, if you end up in cool or cold water in an emergency, use bobbing only as a last resort to save yourself.

- First, you must learn to take a deep breath and submerge while holding your breath. Practice this several times and you'll find that you can remain under the water comfortably for longer periods.
- Next, take a deep breath with your mouth and nose just above the surface of the water, then submerge and breathe out with your mouth and nose just below the surface. Practice this until you can do it easily.
- Bobbing adds body movement to controlled breathing, and it can be done in water that is just slightly over your head. To bob, take a deep breath at the surface, submerge to the bottom, and push off at a forward angle, breathing out as you rise to the surface.

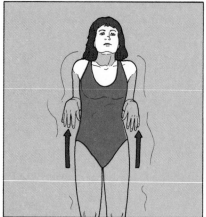

Figure 32
Winging on Back

Floating on Your Back

Many people can float on their backs fairly easily. To help stay afloat, gently move your hands and arms back and forth alongside of your body. This motion is often called "winging" *(Fig. 32)*. Extend your arms along the sides of your body. Draw your fingertips up along the sides of your body and stop at your lowest ribs. Extend your fingertips and hands outward, and push your hands simultaneously in a circular motion toward your feet. Kick only if needed.

Facedown Floating (Survival Floating)

You can use the facedown floating technique called survival floating. It is also called "drownproofing." Remember, if you end up in cool or cold water in an emergency, use facedown floating only as a last resort to save yourself.

When you're facedown in the water, your body tends to swing down into a semivertical position with your head just below the surface. Survival floating is based on this tendency. It was developed to help water accident victims in warm water conserve their energy while they waited to be rescued. Each move you make should be slow and easy.

- While your mouth and nose are above the surface of the water, breathe in, hold your breath, put your face in the water, and let your arms and legs dangle down *(Fig. 33)*. Keep the back of your head level with or just below the surface. Allow yourself to rest in this position for several seconds.
- Slowly lift your arms to about shoulder height and separate your legs with one leg forward and the other back in a stride position *(Fig. 34)*.
- Tilt your head back on your neck to raise your face above the surface, but only high enough for your mouth to clear the water. As you raise your face, breathe out through your mouth or nose *(Fig. 35)*. Keep your eyes open so you can make sure that you don't rise out of the water any farther than you need to in order to breathe.

Figure 33
Survival Floating: Resting Position

Figure 34
Survival Floating: Prepare to Exhale

Figure 35
Survival Floating: Exhale

Figure 36
Survival Floating: Inhale

Figure 37
Survival Floating: Resting Position

- When your mouth clears the water, gently press down with your arms, and in the same motion, straighten your legs and bring them together *(Fig. 36)*. This will help keep your mouth above the water while you take another breath with your mouth.
- Return to the resting position *(Fig. 37)* and repeat these movements.

If you sink too far below the surface while you're in the resting position, press down gently with your arms, or separate and then bring your legs together, as described above, to push yourself up toward the surface.

If you're so buoyant that your body remains on the surface, simply float in a position that's comfortable for you.

Quick review: Learn and practice survival swimming and floating skills. Also practice these techniques fully clothed.

The Submerged Vehicle

In most cases when vehicles plunge into the water, the occupants try frantically to open the doors but can't because of the external water pressure. They begin to panic and are unable to help themselves.

You can help yourself in this kind of emergency if you remain calm and remember the following guidelines:

- Wearing a vehicle safety belt will reduce your chances of being injured when your vehicle hits the water.
- Tests indicate that even a heavy vehicle, such as a station wagon, will float for about 45 seconds after entering the water. During this time, you should try to open the nearest window and leave the car through the window immediately.
- When your vehicle begins to sink, move to the higher end to breathe the trapped air.
- Use one of three routes to escape:
  — Open a window.
  — Open an undamaged door when the water pressure is equal inside and out (when the car is nearly full of water).
  — Break or push out a window. Vehicle windows are usually made of tempered glass.

If you witness a vehicle plunging into the water, get professional rescue assistance. Activate the EMS system.

How to Help Others in an Emergency: Reach, Throw, and Wade

What Happens to People in Water Emergencies?

You've seen it a hundred times in movies, television programs, and cartoons. People who are drowning wave their arms and shout "Help, I'm drowning!" They start slipping under the surface and rising up again. The third time down is their last.

But real water emergencies are not like that. Most people who are drowning are unable to call for help. That's why it's so important for people in and around the water to look out for each other at all times. In this section, you will learn what really happens to people in water emergencies and how to respond safely.

A **tired swimmer** is too tired to get to shore or poolside but is not in any immediate danger.

A **person in distress** is unable to get to safety without assistance, but is able to keep afloat and breathe and may be able to call for help. Someone who's trying to swim but making no progress may be in distress. Two or more persons clinging to a float designed for only one person may be in distress. A person in distress can quickly lose the ability to float and become a drowning person.

A **drowning person** is unable to keep afloat, breathe air, or call for help.

Case History

Most drownings occur within a short distance of safety. Here is one example of how a non-swimmer can save a life, and another example of providing help using a safety device.

A young boy who had taken an American Red Cross water safety course was able to save his sister because of what he learned. A strong ocean current was pulling her away from shore. The boy used an inflated raft to extend his reach to her and pull her back to safety. He rescued his sister without putting himself in danger.

Two young girls were swimming in a lake. One was playing with an inner tube. She hit her head on something in the water, knocking herself unconscious for a moment. When she regained consciousness, she tried to grab the tube. The other young swimmer saw her difficulty, pushed the tube under the victim, and guided her to safety using the tube. She provided the help that was needed with a safety device, rather than grabbing the victim and risking being pulled underwater herself.

Reaching, throwing, and wading are examples of safe, elementary forms of rescue to remember.

Figure 38
Active Drowning Victim

Figure 39
Passive Victim

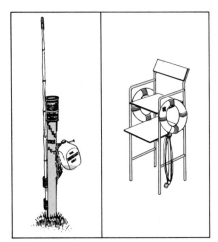

Figure 40
Safety Equipment

An **active drowning victim** may be desperately trying to stay above the surface of the water to get air *(Fig. 38)*. Witnesses to this kind of drowning often say they thought the victim was joking.

A **passive victim** may be floating facedown on or just below the surface of the water, or will sink quietly under the water *(Fig. 39)*.

How Do People Drown?
Generally a drowning victim may rise up and slip below the surface again and again, becoming more tired with each period under the water. If the victim raises his or her arms to signal for help, this action will force the victim farther underwater.

The victim may swallow water or inhale water, which could replace air in the lungs. When this happens, the victim will not be able to call for help because all energy will be directed toward breathing.

Drowning occurs when the victim inhales a large amount of water and suffocates. Drowning also occurs when the victim's airway becomes closed by what is called a *gasp reflex*. This reflex can occur if the victim jumps into very cold water.

A person may be in danger of drowning from a head injury, heart attack, stroke, fainting, overexertion, seizure, or incapacitating cramps, as well as other causes.

How You Can Assist
You can use the reaching, throwing, or wading methods described below to successfully assist someone in a water emergency. In most cases, at least one of these measures will be successful. While you attempt to make the assist, someone in your group should be calling for emergency medical assistance to attend to the victim immediately. **Never overestimate your own ability.**

Equipment
Community pools and outdoor swimming areas that are properly supervised should have the safety equipment described in this section. Hotel and motel pools will usually have one or more pieces of safety equipment, but you should check before you swim *(Fig. 40)*. Recreation and aquatic supply stores carry this equipment for home pool or pond use.

Safety equipment should be kept in plain view at the swimming area. A well-marked safety post is often used for this purpose. The equipment should be easily and quickly accessible.

If you've prepared properly for water recreation, you'll know immediately where the safety equipment is located, how to use it, or how to get help.

Don't Endanger Yourself!

Remember, you can help a victim only if you are in a safe position yourself and if you maintain control of the situation. The reaching, throwing, and wading methods presented in this section will help you to do both.

Swimming out to bring a victim to shore requires special training. If you swim to a victim without this training, you won't be increasing the chances of saving the victim. In fact, you'll only be putting yourself in danger and risking two lives instead of saving one.

Leaping into the water to help someone may seem courageous, but choosing one of the methods described below is much more likely to result in a successful assist.

Reaching

Firmly brace yourself on a deck or pier and reach out to the victim with any object that will extend your reach, such as a pole, a shepherd's crook (a pole with a large hook on the end), an oar or paddle, a tree branch, a shirt, a belt, or a towel *(Figs. 41 and 42)*.

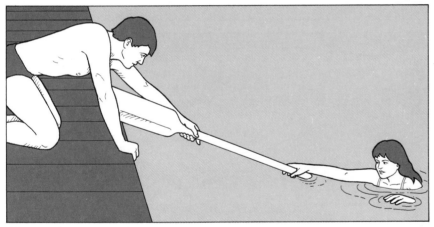

Figure 41
Reach With a Paddle

Figure 42
Shepherd's Crook: Active Victim

When the victim is able to grasp whatever object you extend, slowly and carefully pull him or her to safety.

Reach with a shepherd's crook. If the victim is passive and unable to grab the shepherd's crook, you can use the hook end to encircle the victim's body *(Fig. 43)*. While keeping yourself firmly braced on the deck or pier, place the hook around the victim's chest and under the armpits, carefully pulling him or her to safety.

Figure 43
Shepherd's Crook: Passive Victim

If you see a victim lying on the bottom, you can try to reach him or her with the hook end. Try to encircle the victim's body and pull the victim to the surface. Bring the victim to the edge and turn faceup.

Reach with your arm or leg. To avoid going into the water, lie flat on the pool deck or pier and reach with your arm *(Fig. 44)*. If you are in the water, use one hand to get a firm grasp on the pool ladder, overflow trough, piling, or other secure object, and extend your free hand *(Fig. 45)* or one of your legs *(Fig. 46)* to the victim. Don't let go of your grasp at the water's edge. Do not swim out into the water.

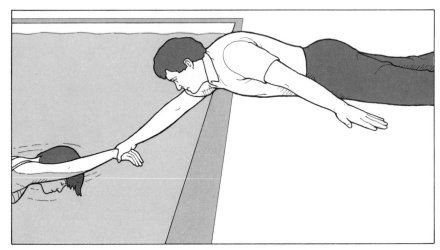

Figure 44
Reach From Deck

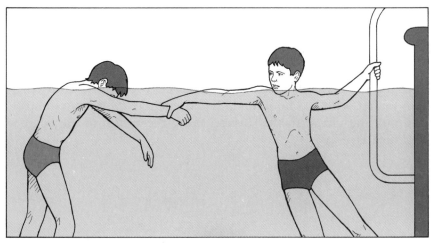

Figure 45
Reach From Pool Ladder

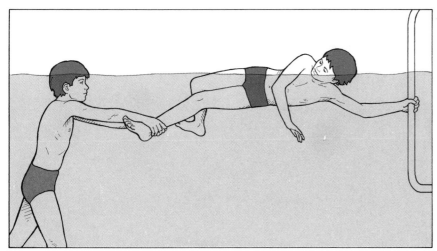

Figure 46
Leg Extension From Ladder

Throwing

You can throw a heaving line, a ring buoy, a throw bag, a rescue tube, or a homemade heaving device so the victim can grab it and be pulled carefully to safety.

How to Throw

- Get into a position that is safe and allows you to maintain your balance *(Fig. 47)*.
- Bend your knees.
- Step on the nonthrowing end of the line.
- Aim your throw *(Fig. 48)* so the device will fall just beyond the victim but within reach *(Fig. 49)*.

Figure 47
Aim Ring Buoy

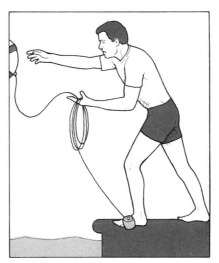

Figure 48
Throw Ring Buoy

Figure 49
Ring Buoy Position After Throw

Figure 51
Heaving Line

Figure 52
Throw Heaving Line

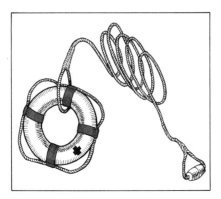

Figure 53
Ring Buoy

- Throw the device so the drift from the wind or current will bring it back within the victim's reach.
- Slowly pull the victim, who is now grasping the device, to safety. Lean your body weight away from the victim as you pull *(Fig. 50)*.

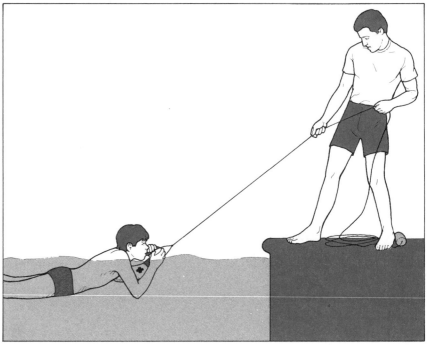

Figure 50
Pull Victim to Safety

Heaving Line *(Fig. 51)*

The line should float and should be white, yellow, or another highly visible color. A floatable, weighted object on the throwing end will give the throw more accuracy *(Fig. 52)*.

Ring Buoy *(Fig. 53)*

This is made of buoyant cork, kapok, cellular foam, or plastic-covered material. The buoy should have a towline or lightweight line with a "lemon" or other object at the end to prevent the line from slipping out from under your foot when you throw the ring buoy. The buoy and coiled line should be hung on the safety post in such a way that anyone can quickly grasp them and throw to an individual in trouble.

Throw Bag *(Fig. 54)*

This is a small and very useful rescue device made from a nylon bag with 50 to 75 feet of floating line attached. A foam disk at the bottom of the bag gives it shape and prevents it from sinking.

Rescue Tube *(Fig. 55)*

This is a tube made of vinyl foam, approximately 3 inches by 6 inches by 40 inches, with a 6-foot towline and web shoulder strap.

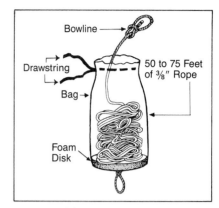

Figure 54
Throw Bag

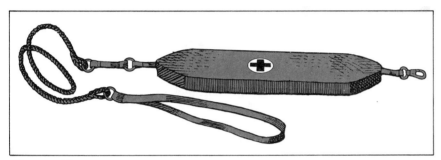

Figure 55
Rescue Tube

If the victim is struggling in the water within 6 to 8 feet of the shore or the edge of the pool, the 6-foot towline and the additional 2 feet of shoulder strap will be long enough to make an assist. Clip the ends of the tube together to make an improvised ring buoy. Throw the tube with one hand and hold onto the webbing loop with the other *(Fig. 56)*. When the victim grasps the tube, carefully pull in the line and the victim to safety.

Figure 56
Throw Rescue Tube

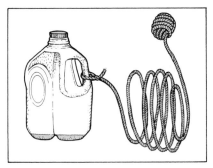

Figure 57
Jug With Line

Homemade Heaving Device *(Fig. 57)*
You can make a homemade heaving device by putting a half-inch of water into a gallon plastic container, sealing the container, and attaching approximately 50 to 75 feet of floating line to the handle. The water in the jug adds weight to help direct the throw *(Fig. 58)*.

Wading

If you can wade in the water without danger from currents or objects on the bottom, wade in with a buoyant object and extend it to the victim *(Fig. 59)*. For this kind of assist, use a rescue tube, a ring buoy, a buoyant cushion, a kickboard, or a PFD. If you do not have a buoyant object, you may extend your reach with a tree branch, pole, or other object to the victim *(Fig. 60)*.

Figure 58
Throw Jug

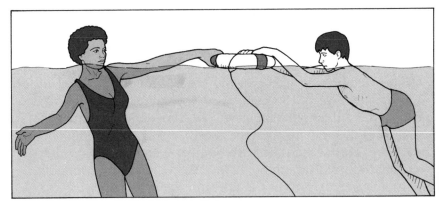

Figure 59
Wade With Ring Buoy

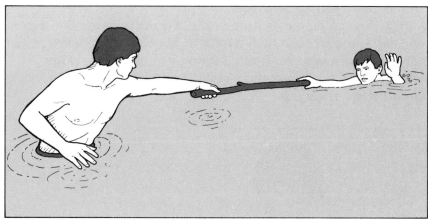

Figure 60
Wade With Extension

You can use the safety device for support in the water, and the victim can grasp the other side of it. You can then pull the victim to safety, or you can let go of the safety device and tell the victim to start kicking with it toward safety.

Always keep the safety device between you and the victim. If the victim should panic and grab you, you would be in danger of drowning also. Keeping the safety device between you and the victim will help prevent the victim from grabbing you.

Figure 61
Free-Floating Support

Figure 62
Throw a Floating Support

The Free-Floating Support

A PFD, floating plastic jug, inner tube, air mattress, paddle, water ski, and a tree branch are examples of free-floating supports. Carefully push or toss a free-floating support to the victim *(Figs. 61 and 62)*, and encourage the victim to grasp the support and kick toward safety *(Fig. 63)*.

Figure 63
Float With Support

Talking to the Victim

With your instructions, a person in distress may be able to help you make the assist. Tell the victim that help is on the way and give instructions on what to do, such as grabbing the heaving line or rescue buoy.

Ask the victim to try to move toward you by kicking or stroking. Some victims have made their way to safety by themselves with the calm and encouraging assistance of someone calling to them.

Rescue Breathing for Victims of Water Emergencies

You may need to perform rescue breathing for the victim of a water emergency. This procedure is much more difficult in the water than on land because you must support the victim while you perform the rescue breathing techniques. For complete information on rescue breathing, contact your local American Red Cross chapter about CPR and first aid courses and materials such as *Rescue Breathing and Choking Supplement* (Stock No. 329286). See the poster *When Breathing Stops* in the Appendix.

Rescue Breathing in Shallow Water

You may need to perform rescue breathing while you and the victim are in shallow water. If the victim's head is to your left, slide your right arm between the victim's right arm and body. If the victim's head is to your right, slide your left arm between the victim's left arm and body. To keep the victim's head above the surface, you may need to use your supporting arm while holding onto a rescue tube, ring buoy, or pool edge *(Fig. 64)* to support the victim's back. Bring your other arm over to position the victim's head, pinch the nostrils, and proceed with rescue breathing.

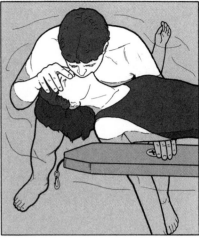

Figure 64
Rescue Breathing in Shallow Water

Case History

Cold water presents more danger than many people realize. Even being a good swimmer may not protect you in a cold water accident.

On a fall day, some students went fishing in a small boat on a lake; the star quarterback for the football team was among them. The wind was blowing and the temperature was 50° to 60°F. The water was extremely cold.

The boat started to leak and then began to sink. Two of the passengers made it safely to shore, but the star quarterback, a very good swimmer, panicked at being unexpectedly immersed in the extremely cold water. He was unable to swim to safety and he drowned. No one had taken a personal flotation device (PFD) on the trip.

The students would have been wise to stay on shore. At the least, they should have checked the boat carefully before going out, and each passenger should have worn a PFD.

Exposure to Cold Water

Falling off a dock, breaking through ice on a lake, being thrown into the water as your boat swerves—these accidents can lead to the danger of immersion hypothermia, or exposure to cold water.

Hypothermia refers to a low body temperature, specifically a low core temperature (temperature of the vital organs). Hypothermia occurs when cold or cool temperatures cause the body to lose heat faster than it can produce it, and the temperature of the vital organs (body core temperature) falls below normal.

Cold water is defined as being 70°F or colder, but hypothermia can occur in water that is in the 80°F range. As a general rule, if the water *feels* cold, it *is* cold.

What Happens if You Fall into Cold Water?
- The temperature of your skin drops quickly, as does the temperature of the blood in your arms and legs.
- You may initially have difficulty breathing, and you may gradually become unable to use your hands.
- The temperature of your heart, brain, and other vital organs gradually drops.
- You begin shivering.
- You may become unconscious. If your temperature drops further, you can die of heart failure.

How Long Can You Survive in Cold Water?
Survival length depends on your body size and type, your age, and what you're wearing. Large people and people with more body fat may survive longer. Children are smaller and have less fat, so they are affected more quickly by hypothermia. Elderly people are also at greater risk.

Wearing a personal flotation device (PFD) increases your survival time significantly, and gives rescuers more time to find and help you. A PFD can provide extra insulation and keep your face out of the water, which will slow down heat loss.

Guidelines for Prevention of Hypothermia
- When you're around cold water—playing, working, hunting, fishing—remember that cold water can be a danger even if you don't intend to go in.
- Participate in water activities only when and where you can get help quickly in an emergency.
- Wear a Coast Guard–approved PFD while boating. Have PFDs available whenever you're around cold water.
- If you're going to be around water in cooler weather, wear rain gear or wool clothing. Wool acts as an insulator even when it's wet.
- Wear layers of clothes.

- Carry matches in a waterproof container. You may need to build a fire to warm up after a fall into cold water.
- Don't drink alcohol, thinking that it will warm you. Alcohol actually increases loss of body heat.

Are Winter Clothes a Danger in the Water?

People who fall into the water while wearing winter clothes, especially heavy boots or waders, usually panic, thinking they'll sink immediately to the bottom. But winter clothes can actually help you float. Also, heavy clothing has been shown to help in delaying hypothermia. Tight-fitting foam vests and flotation jackets with foam insulation can double survival time.

If you fall into the water wearing a snowmobile suit or other heavy winter clothes, air will be trapped in the clothes, and you'll quickly rise to the surface. Simply lie back, spread your arms and legs out, and use a "winging" motion to propel yourself toward safety *(Fig. 65)*. (See the section Floating on Your Back, page 40.)

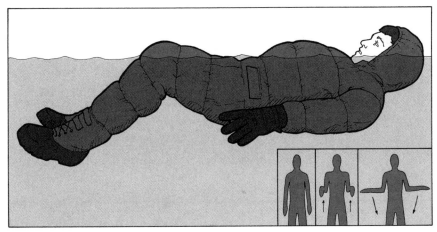

Figure 65
Winging While Clothed

Hip boots, waders, and rubber boots often trap air during falls into water. If you relax and bend your knees, the trapped air in your boots may begin to bring you up to the surface very quickly *(Fig. 66)*.

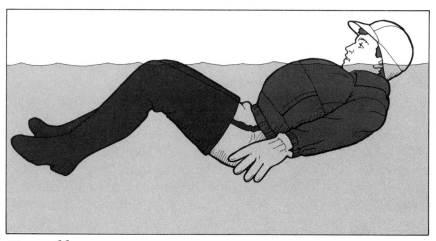

Figure 66
Back Float: Trapped Air

While on your back you can float in a tuck position. Bring your knees up toward your chest, let your hips drop, and keep your head up and back. Then paddle backwards with your hands toward safety.

You can also float on your front. Keep your head raised and bend your knees. Paddle forward with your arms in the water *(Fig. 67)*.

Figure 67
Front Float: Trapped Air

In cold water, you must decide whether you'll try to reach safety or whether you'll float and wait for help. You're likely to find that you can't swim as far in cold water as you can in warm water. It is important to only use a swimming stroke with underwater arm recovery. If you can get to safety with a few swimming strokes, do so. If not, float quietly and wait for rescue.

Note that treading water chills the body faster than remaining still with a PFD in the water. In cold water, treading water is a last resort to use only if you are unable to remain afloat any other way.

Remember that when you reach safety, your clothing will be heavy with water. Stand for a moment and allow some of the water to drain away before you try to move.

Figure 68
H.E.L.P. Position

If You Fall into Cold Water With a PFD

Even if the air temperature is warm, you should wear a PFD when around cold water, even if you are a good swimmer. Should you fall into cold water—

- Keep your face and head above the surface. If you've been in a boating accident, you may be able to climb up onto your cap- sized boat to get more of your body out of the water.

- Keep all your clothing on, including your hat. Even clothing that's wet will help you retain body heat.

- Swim toward safety if a current is carrying you toward some danger. Unless you must swim away immediately, float on your back and go downstream feetfirst until you slow your breathing rate. Breathe normally for a few seconds before you begin swimming to shore.

- If you are not in immediate danger, but are some distance from shore, remain still and let your PFD support you until help arrives.

Figure 69
Huddle Position

If You're Waiting to be Rescued

There are two positions that you can maintain in the water with a PFD. Because both these positions are somewhat difficult to main- tain, you may want to practice them in warm shallow water. Always practice under the supervision of someone who has the water safety skills to help you if you have difficulty.

- **H.E.L.P. (Heat Escape Lessening Posture).** Draw your knees up toward your chest, keep your face forward and out of the water, hold your upper arms at your sides, and fold your lower arms across your chest *(Fig. 68)*. Do not use the H.E.L.P. posi- tion in swift river currents or white water.

- **Huddle** (for two or more persons). Put your arms over one another's shoulders so the sides of your chests are together, sandwiching any children between adults *(Fig. 69)*.

If You Fall into Cold Water Without a PFD

- Look around for a log or other floating object to support you. If you've been in a boating accident, you may be able to hold on-to the capsized boat.
- Raise as much of your body as possible out of the water. In particular, keep your face and head above the surface. If there are waves, turn your back to them to help keep water out of your face.
- Keep all your clothing on, including your hat. Even clothing that's wet will help you retain body heat.
- Don't splash around trying to warm up. Your body will generate more heat, but it won't stay with you. Splashing will only increase blood circulation in your arms and legs, and can drain what energy you might have.
- Swim only if you are close enough to shore to reach it safely. The distance you'll be able to swim will depend on your swimming ability, the amount of insulation you're wearing, and the water conditions. But you're likely to find that you can't swim as far in cold water as you can in warm water. And it isn't easy to judge distance, especially under emergency conditions. Even if you're a good swimmer, when water temperatures are about 50°F or lower, it will be difficult for you to reach shore.

Quick review: If you fall into cold water while wearing a PFD, hold still and wait for help unless you can get to shore with a few swimming strokes. If you fall into water without a PFD, hold onto the boat or look around for a log or other floating object to support you.

Helping Yourself Once You're Ashore

Remember these tips once you've reached safety after falling in cold water:

- Change into dry clothes if possible. If not, take off your wet clothes, wring them out, and put them back on. Even damp clothes will help insulate you, especially if they're wool.
- Get inside a building.
- If possible, get heat from a warm room, a warm shower or bath, or start a fire to warm quickly.
- As soon as possible, drink warm fluids such as hot broth or soup. Avoid beverages that are caffeinated or alcoholic.
- When you've warmed up, begin walking to safety if you know where you are and where you can get help. If you don't know what direction to go in, stay by the fire and wait for rescue. Smoke from the fire will help rescuers find you.
- If you are unable to build a fire and you don't know what direction to go in, protect yourself from the wind and cold as much as possible while you wait for help.

Helping Victims of Cold Water Exposure

In all cases, act quickly. These symptoms will tell you when some-one has suffered cold water exposure:

- Shivering
- Weakness
- Confusion
- Slurred speech
- Semi-consciousness or unconsciousness

When you're helping others, remember that cold water exposure is a severe physical shock. Treat victims very gently and monitor their breathing carefully.

Helping a Conscious Victim Once Ashore

As soon as possible, take the victim to a dry, sheltered area, and remove the wet clothing. Put the victim in dry clothes, blankets, a sleeping bag, or any covering that will provide insulation. If possible, start a fire to warm up the victim.

If the facilities are available, help the victim sit under a warm shower or in a warm bath. The water temperature should be warm but not hot. If you use a bath, keep the victim's arms and legs out of the water to raise the core, or deep body, temperature first.

If you use a shower, have the victim sit on a chair in the shower, in case the victim becomes faint.

Give the victim warm fluids, but never give drinks containing alcohol or caffeine. Stay with the victim until he or she is warm and acts normally.

Get medical assistance if possible.

Helping an Unconscious Victim Once Ashore

If you are positive the victim has no pulse or respiration, and only if you have been properly trained, give CPR (cardiopulmonary resuscitation).

If or when the victim has a pulse, try to prevent any further heat loss. Move the victim to a dry, sheltered area. Remove wet clothing gently. Place dry blankets over and under the victim. Providing some type of heat source, such as a fire, will also help.

Medical personnel will use special methods of restoring the victim's body warmth. Even victims who have had no life signs have been revived with prompt medical attention—so act quickly!

Quick review: Help conscious victims by rewarming them quickly. Help unconscious victims by getting medical attention immediately and doing CPR if needed, and only if you are qualified.

Ice Safety

You can safely enjoy outdoor ice sports and activities by learning about ice formation and by taking a few simple precautions to protect yourself.

What Makes Ice Unsafe?
- Springs and fast-moving water
- Wind and wave action
- Waterfowl and schooling fish
- Decomposing material in the water
- Water bubblers (these are devices designed to keep the water around boat docks from freezing thick)
- Material in rivers and lakes that is discharged from industrial sites
- Objects protruding through the ice, such as tree stumps

Preventing Ice Accidents
- Check the ice thickness before you go out. For maximum safety, ice should be solid and at least four inches thick. In some areas, you can get information about ice thickness from conservation departments or local weather stations. Remember, ice thickness may not be the same over an entire area.
- Note that solid, four-inch-thick ice is generally safe to walk on. It is *not* thick enough to drive a vehicle on.
- Remember that the more people on the ice, the thicker the ice must be for safety.
- Choose smaller, shallower, and slower moving bodies of water for ice activities; the ice may be more solid.
- Look for objects that are sticking up through the ice and mark them as hazards.
- Don't go out on ice that has recently frozen, thawed, and then refrozen. This happens in the spring and early winter as temperatures change often. Wait until the outside temperature has stayed below freezing so that at least four inches of solid ice forms over the entire area you'll be using.
- Always stay with at least one other person. (Remember, more people require thicker ice for safety.)
- Tell someone where you will be and when you intend to return.
- Wear warm clothing. Wool is the best material for holding warm air next to your body and for providing insulation, even if it gets wet.
- Have something available to throw or extend to a person who needs help—PFDs, a rope with a weighted end, a long tree branch, a wooden pole, a plastic jug with a line attached.
- Carry matches in a waterproof container. You may need to build a fire to warm up after a fall into cold water.

Quick review: Ice thickness is affected by many factors. Make sure the ice is thick and solid before going on it. Have an emergency throwing or reaching device ready.

What to Do if the Ice Cracks or Starts to Give Way Under You

* Lie down immediately, spreading out your arms and legs to distribute your weight evenly. Do not stand up until you reach safety.
* Crawl or roll to safety, keeping your arms and legs spread out as much as possible.

What to Do if You Fall Through the Ice

* Resist the urge to quickly climb out on the ice. It may be weak around the area where you've fallen in.
* Quickly begin to float on your stomach. Bend your knees to help trap some air in your pant legs and boots.
* Reach forward onto the unbroken ice—but do not push down on the ice. Use a breaststroke kick or another kick to push yourself farther onto the ice.
* Don't stand up when you get on the ice. Crawl or roll away from the break area, keeping your arms and legs spread out as much as possible.
* Have your companion throw or extend an emergency device to you if you need one. Remember not to stand on the ice.

Review the section Exposure to Cold Water, page 58, for the steps to take when you are safely out of the water.

What to Do if Someone Else Falls Through the Ice

- Do not go onto the ice yourself. The ice may give way, and there will be two victims in the water instead of one.
- From a secure place on shore, extend or throw an emergency device to the victim—tree branch, pole, PFD, weighted rope, inner tube, plastic jug with line—anything that will support the victim until you can get help *(Fig. 70)*. Act quickly. Within minutes, the victim will lose the ability to grasp the object.
- If you can do so safely, pull the victim to shore. If not, make sure the victim has grasped the emergency device for support, and get help immediately.

Figure 70
Ice Rescue With Branch

Review the section Exposure to Cold Water, page 58, for the steps to take to help the victim.

4 *Boating Safety*

Boating Safety

Case History

Boating is great fun—when it's done safely. Drinking while boating and operating boats recklessly lead to danger.

Several young people in two motorboats were enjoying a day on the river. They were both moving fast when one boat suddenly rammed into the side of the other.

A 16-year-old was thrown into the water. She died later of brain damage and pneumonia. A 26-year-old was also thrown into the water, and his body was recovered a week later. Other members of the party suffered wounds and broken bones.

Investigators found many empty beer cans and wine bottles in the boats. The accident report concluded that the young people were racing their boats to see how close they could come to each other head-on.

The young people shouldn't have been drinking while boating, and those driving the boats should not have engaged in such a dangerous activity.

Small craft are boats that are 16 feet or less in length. Although they can provide very enjoyable water recreation, boating accidents happen all too frequently with small craft. The U.S. Coast Guard reports that U.S. waterways are second only to highways as the scene of transportation deaths.

Everyone who will be boating should know how to operate a boat safely and how to swim. And regardless of their swimming abilities, all boat passengers should wear a Coast Guard–approved personal flotation device (PFD) at all times.

You should take a course or lessons in boat handling so you understand—

- Differences among types of craft.
- Effects of wind, water conditions, and weather.
- How to use boating equipment.
- Navigation rules and safe boat handling.
- Boat maintenance.
- Emergency procedures.

To find out about boating courses in your area, check with your local American Red Cross, the U.S. Power Squadron, the U.S. Coast Guard Auxiliary, the United States Yacht Racing Union, the American Canoe Association, or area marinas and recreational facilities. (See the Appendix for addresses.)

Quick review: Before you go boating, learn how to handle boats properly and safely. When you're boating, wear a Coast Guard–approved PFD at all times.

Drinking and Boating Don't Mix

The U.S. Coast Guard says that more than 50 percent of the drownings from boat accidents are alcohol related. And it doesn't take much drinking to make a big difference.

Here's how alcohol affects your boating ability, according to the U.S. Coast Guard:

- Alcohol affects your balance. It can make you more likely to tumble off the boat.
- Alcohol makes you less able to stay warm—even though you might feel warm when you take your first drink.
- Alcohol affects your judgment.
- Alcohol slows your movements and impairs your vision.
- Alcohol can reduce your swimming abilities, even if you're an excellent swimmer.

Don't endanger yourself, your family, and friends. Stay sober and free of drugs while you're boating. If someone who has been drinking or using drugs offers you a boat ride, don't be embarrassed to refuse. Don't let social pressure force you into a possibly fatal mistake!

Choosing a Place for Boating

- Use small boats only in areas that are well away from swimming areas.
- Different kinds of small boats should have separate docking facilities for safer maneuvering while boats are approaching or leaving the dock.
- Stay a minimum of 100 feet from diving flags that indicate when divers are underwater.
- Before you go boating, check weather reports from the local newspaper, radio, or television—or telephone the U.S. Coast Guard.
- Obey storm or gale warnings, small craft advisories, and warning flags *(Fig. 71)*. Such warnings are provided to alert boaters to weather and water conditions that might be hazardous.

Equipping Your Boat

There are federal and state requirements for boating equipment. Check specific requirements for the type of boat you'll be operating. The nearest installation of the U.S. Coast Guard, Coast Guard Auxiliary, or U.S. Power Squadron will be able to give you full information.

You shouldn't stop at the minimum requirements for equipment. Consider the following list of equipment:

- Coast Guard–approved PFD for each person aboard, kept in good condition and readily available. Nonswimmers *must wear* PFDs.
- Sound-signaling device—whistle, horn, or bell.
- Visual distress signaling devices—flares or flags for daytime, flares or electric lights for nighttime. Check the U.S. Coast Guard requirements and recommendations.
- Extra oars or paddle to maneuver the boat or to extend to an accident victim in the water.
- Fire extinguisher.
- Running lights.
- Anchor.
- Extra line.
- Throw bag.
- First aid kit.
- Bailing device.
- Flashlight.
- Tool kit and spare parts for the boat.
- Charts.
- Compass.
- Radio for listening to weather reports.
- Extra throwable PFDs.

This equipment should be checked frequently for wear and damage. Each piece of equipment should be stored in a well-ventilated place after each use.

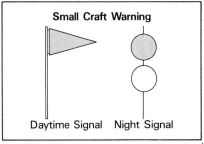

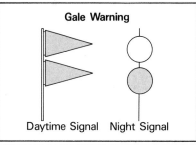

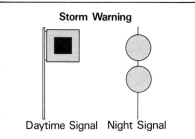

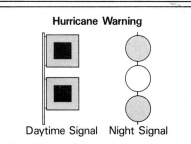

Figure 71
Weather Warning Flags

Boating Safety

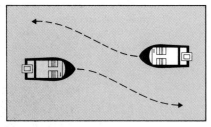

Figure 72
Meeting

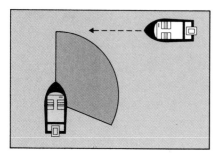

Figure 73
Crossing

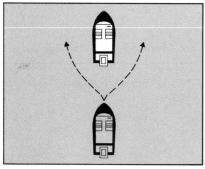

Figure 74
Passing

The PFD: It's Really a Lifesaver!

The U.S. Coast Guard requires that each boat carry one PFD for each person on board. You shouldn't stop at the minimum requirement. Each passenger should wear the PFD at all times.

The Coast Guard has approved various types of PFDs for use on recreational boats, which are listed in the section Personal Flotation Devices (PFDs), page 7. When you choose a PFD—

- Make sure it's the proper size.
- Practice putting it on in shallow water and swimming with it.
- Always practice with a companion.
- Wear it at all times while boating. If there's an emergency, you won't have to worry about putting it on and you may not have time to do so.

Navigation Rules

Boat operators must learn and obey navigation rules, also known as "rules of the road." These navigation rules are designed to keep boating safe and enjoyable.

The navigation rules are established by a committee appointed by the U.S. Congress and are administered by the U.S. Coast Guard. Your nearest Coast Guard installation can provide you complete information on these rules. Courses offered by U.S. Power Squadron, U.S. Coast Guard Auxiliary, and United States Yacht Racing Union also provide information and training on navigation rules.

Right of Way

The rules require boats with motors to give the right of way to boats that are under sail or being rowed or paddled—the one exception being when a sailboat overtakes a motorboat.

Even if your boat has the right of way, you should still operate it carefully and responsibly. Always make clear to other boat operators what you're going to do by using the signals specified in the navigation rules.

Meeting

When you are approaching another boat head-on or nearly so, keep to your right, just as you do with automobiles *(Fig. 72)*.

Crossing

The boat on the right has the right of way. The boat on the left must slow down, change course, or pass behind the other boat. The boat on the left should have prepared to stop or reverse course to avoid a collision *(Fig. 73)*.

Passing

The boat being passed has the right of way. The boat that's passing may pass on either side after proper signals have been exchanged, such as one horn blast to signal passing on the right, two to pass on the left. The passing boat must keep clear of the boat being passed *(Fig. 74)*.

Quick review: Wear a Coast Guard – approved PFD. Make sure your boat is properly equipped. Know the navigation rules and cooperate with other boat operators for everyone's safety.

Keeping Your Boat Balanced

Don't carry more people than recommended. Check the U.S. Coast Guard capacity information attached to your boat *(Fig. 75)*.

Trim the boat—that is, balance the weight from side to side *(Fig. 76)* and from front to back *(Fig. 77)*.

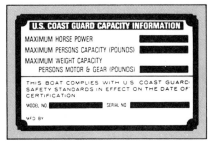

Figure 75
Boat Capacity Plate

Figure 76
Trim: Side to Side

Figure 77
Trim: Bow to Stern

Getting Aboard

Start your boating recreation safely by knowing how to properly board (how to get on) and debark (how to get off).

- Know the parts of a boat or canoe *(Fig. 78)*.
- Wear nonskid deck shoes.
- Watch for boat wakes or waves that may throw you off balance.
- Alert those already on board that you are about to board (or debark).
- Have another person hold and help stabilize the boat while you board.
- Be careful not to step on equipment.
- Keep your weight low to the bottom of the boat to keep the boat stable.

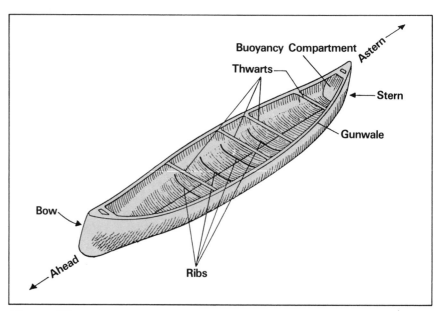

Figure 78
Parts of a Canoe

At a Dock

Make sure the boat is tied at the front (bow) and the back (stern), with the lines snug but not so tight that they keep the boat from settling when weight is added.

Step aboard as near as possible to the center of the boat. Reach down to grasp the side (gunwale) of the boat as you shift your weight to the foot resting in the boat. Then bring the trailing foot aboard *(Fig. 79)*.

If the dock is much higher than the boat, sit on the dock and then step into the boat.

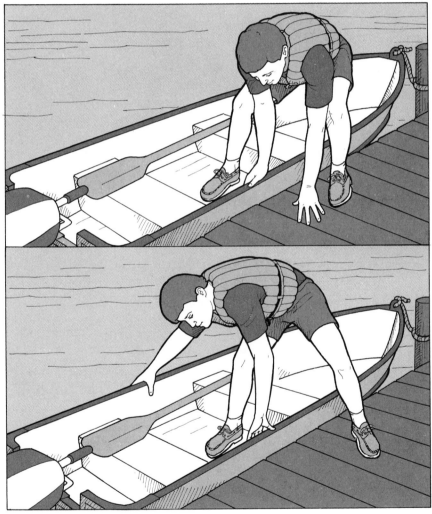

Figure 79
Board at Dock

At a Beach or Shoreline

Make sure the boat is floating. Step over the bow or stern while you grasp the sides with both hands. Shift your weight to the foot in the boat. Keep your weight low to the bottom of the boat as you bring your trailing foot aboard *(Fig. 80)*.

Figure 80
Board at Shoreline

To Debark

Simply do the reverse of the steps to board. Keeping your weight low, step ashore or onto the dock, carefully shift your weight to the leading foot, and then bring in your trailing foot.

Changing Positions

If passengers need to change positions in small boats—
- Only one person should move at a time.
- Try to keep the weight low and as near the center of the boat as possible.
- Keep the boat trimmed, that is, balance the weight of one passenger against the weight of another.
- If waves are heavy, change positions only if it is necessary to correct the balance of weight.

Quick review: Balance of weight is critical to boating safety. Make sure your boat is properly trimmed at all times. Never drink alcohol while operating a boat.

Exiting and Reentering the Marina

Follow the rules governing right of way. Always travel at low speed, producing a small wake, when you're near docks, piers, or congested boat ramp areas. Watch out for swimmers, other boats, and objects in the water.

If your boat capsizes or swamps—
- Stay with the boat. It will probably float and support you. Rescuers will be able to find you more easily.
- Leave the boat only if there is a fire or if the boat is headed toward a waterfall, dam, or other hazard.
- Hold onto the hull and wait for rescue. If there are two or more passengers, arrange yourselves along each side of the hull. If someone needs to rest, you can grasp each other's wrists across the keel.
- Enter a swamped boat *(Fig. 81)* and hand-paddle to shore *(Fig. 82)*.

Figure 81
Enter a Swamped Boat

Figure 82
Hand-Paddle a Swamped Boat

Figure 83
Canoe Reentry: Place Hands on Bottom

Figure 84
Canoe Reentry: Kick Feet to Surface

Figure 85
Canoe Reentry: Rotate Hips

If you fall out of a canoe, or the canoe swamps—
- Stay with the canoe. It will probably float and support you. Rescuers will be able to find you more easily.
- Leave the canoe if it is headed toward a waterfall, dam, or other hazard.
- If the canoe is upright and not completely swamped, place your hands at the bottom of the canoe *(Fig. 83)*.
- Kick vigorously to raise your hips to the gunwale *(Fig. 84)*.
- Rotate your hips to sit on the bottom of the canoe, and bring your legs into the canoe *(Fig. 85)*. Paddle or hand-paddle to shore.

- If the canoe is completely swamped, lie across middle of the canoe to keep the canoe from turning side to side *(Fig. 86)*.
- Once the canoe is stablilized, rotate your body *(Fig. 87)*.
- Turn to a sitting position and hand-paddle to safety *(Fig. 88)*.

What to Do if Someone in the Water Needs Assistance

Review what you learned in the section How to Help Others in an Emergency, page 43.

Since you've equipped your boat properly, you'll have an emergency device for reaching or throwing—a paddle, an extra PFD, a ring buoy, or some other safety item.

Remember that your boat can become a hazard to the victim, particularly if the boat has a motor. If you approach a victim in your boat, do so against the wind or current, so your boat won't be pushed into the victim. If your boat is motorized, turn the motor off at least three boat lengths away from the victim.

You can throw a flotation device to the victim, so that the victim can paddle to safety. Or you can extend or throw a device that has a line attached and then tow the victim to your boat, so that he or she can come aboard. You can also reach out to the victim with your hand to pull the victim toward the boat *(Fig. 89)*. Keep the boat trimmed. Have other passengers move to the opposite side from where the victim is coming aboard and stabilize the craft.

Figure 86
Swamped Canoe: Stabilize Canoe

Figure 87
Swamped Canoe: Rotate Body

Figure 88
Swamped Canoe: Hand-Paddle

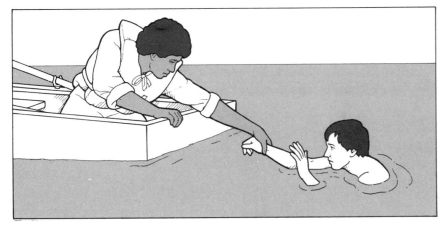

Figure 89
Reaching Assist From Boat

If the victim needs assistance, have one passenger help the victim out of the water and into a "jackknife" position over the edge of the boat. Then swing the victim's legs into the boat *(Fig. 90)*.

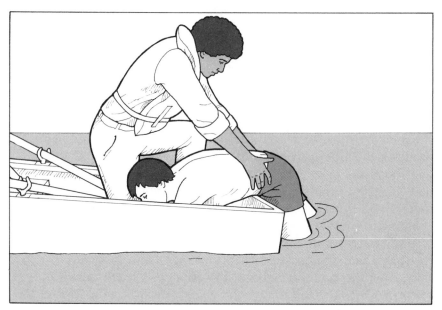

Figure 90
Jackknife Position Into Boat

You can use a variety of ways to signal others about an emergency.
- Signal to others with four or more short blasts from an air horn.
- Communicate an emergency with a two-way radio.
- Wave your arms in a horizon-to-horizon motion.

Quick review: If you see someone in trouble in the water, remember that you can offer the most help from a safe position in your boat. Extend or throw an emergency device to the victim.

Appendixes

The Emergency Medical Services (EMS) System

Throughout this course, you have learned how important it is for you and your community's EMS system to work together in order to give the victim of a medical emergency the best chance of survival.

This appendix explains what an EMS system is and how a victim of injury or sudden illness "enters" the system and what should happen when EMS personnel arrive at the scene of the emergency. At the end of this appendix there is a list of questions to help you learn more about your community's EMS system.

What Is an Emergency Medical Services (EMS) System?

To save a life in a life-threatening situation, two things must happen. Emergency care must be started right away by a trained bystander, and this care must be continued and enhanced by EMS personnel when they arrive. If no one with first aid training is nearby to begin emergency care immediately, or if the community's EMS system cannot quickly provide the right kind of help, then a victim's chances of survival may be greatly reduced.

Components of an EMS System

Providing the victim with the right care at the right time is not an easy task. Although most communities have some way of sending medical help to victims of sudden illness or accidents, this help may not include everything that the victim needs and may not arrive in time to give the victim the best chance of surviving. Your community's ability to get the right help to the victim as quickly as possible requires both planning and resources. EMS systems that do this effectively usually have the following parts:

1. **Trained citizens.** Trained citizens can give first aid and alert the EMS system that a medical emergency has happened.

2. **Trained personnel.** To provide the best help quickly, an EMS system has specially trained personnel. These may include emergency medical technicians (EMTs), emergency medical technician-paramedics (paramedics), first responders (police, fire fighters), emergency dispatchers, and hospital emergency department physicians and nurses trained in emergency medicine.

3. **Special equipment.** Different situations and medical needs require specialized medical, rescue, and transportation equipment.

4. **Communications systems.** How well the EMS system works depends on how quickly citizens can alert the system that an emergency has happened, and how quickly the dispatcher can get the appropriate emergency personnel to the scene. Communications systems are also important because EMS personnel often need to communicate with the hospital emergency department as they care for the victim at the scene of the emergency and on the way to the hospital.
5. **Management and evaluation.** An EMS system needs a management structure that includes administration and coordination of all parts of the system, medical supervision and direction, and ongoing evaluation and research.

The Responsibilities of the Rescuer in the EMS System

In order for the victim of a medical emergency to receive care from the EMS system, the victim must "enter the system." This means that the EMS system must be told about the emergency, and care should be given until EMS personnel arrive. These important first steps are generally performed by a citizen rescuer.

There are three things that you must do to make sure that a victim enters the EMS system with the best chance of survival:
1. **Recognize that a medical emergency has happened.**
2. **Give first aid.**
3. **Phone the EMS system for help.**

How an EMS System Responds to a Call for Help

In many communities, a dispatcher will answer your call. The dispatcher is very important in making sure that the victim gets the right care immediately. In some systems, this person has special training to get specific information from the caller and to know which personnel and equipment to send to the scene. Some dispatchers can also give first aid instructions to the caller over the phone when it is necessary.

Basic Life Support and Advanced Life Support

The information you provide to the EMS dispatcher is important. It will help determine the type of care that the dispatcher sends to the scene of an emergency. The dispatcher may send either an ambulance capable of continuing basic life support, or an ambulance capable of delivering advanced life support. The care sent will depend on the needs of the victim and the services available in your community.

First Responder

When a dispatcher receives a call for emergency medical help the dispatcher will select the type of care that is needed and send the appropriate personnel. This may include police, fire, rescue, and ambulance personnel, depending on the type of emergency and the resources available at the time of the call.

In many communities, police and fire fighters may arrive at the scene before the ambulance because they are often located closer to the scene of the emergency. If you have been caring for a victim, the first responder may take over or ask you to assist. On the other hand, the first responder may tell you to continue care while he or she attends to other problems at the scene. It is important that you do not stop caring for a victim until the first responder takes over. You should expect the first responder to ask you for information about the victim. Information that you have gained from your primary and secondary surveys of the victim may be valuable to first responders, EMTs, paramedics, and to the hospital staff who will care for the victim later.

When the Ambulance Arrives

When the ambulance arrives, the EMTs or paramedics will take over responsibility for care of the victim and will provide additional medical care. Their goal is to begin to stabilize the victim's condition (correct life-threatening problems) at the scene. Once this has been done, the EMS personnel will prepare the victim for transport to the appropriate hospital emergency department, and they will continue caring for the victim on the way. When the ambulance arrives at the hospital, the EMS personnel will transfer responsibility for care of the victim to the emergency room staff.

Assessing Your Community's Emergency Medical Services (EMS) System

With a better idea of the different parts and responsibilities of a community emergency medical services system, you will be better able to assess the emergency medical services offered by your own community.

Your answers to the following questions will help you evaluate the services that your community provides. The questions to which you answer YES will show you the strengths of your community's EMS system. The questions to which you answer NO will point out areas where your community's EMS system could be strengthened. As a citizen and a taxpayer, your support of your community's EMS system is as important as your knowing how to perform first aid.

EMS Questionnaire

The following questions reflect the EMS standards set forth in the Emergency Medical Services Systems Act of 1973, the federal EMS legislation.

1. Are regularly scheduled CPR and first aid classes, open to the public, offered in your community? YES _____ NO _____

2. Does your community have a 9-1-1 emergency number for EMS, fire, and police? YES _____ NO _____

3. Do your local schools certify students in first aid and CPR? YES _____ NO _____

4. Are local police officers trained and certified in American Red Cross First Aid or in the U.S. Department of Transportation First Responder training? YES _____ NO _____

5. Is your local ambulance service staffed by EMTs? YES _____ NO _____

6. Does your local ambulance service regularly leave the station to answer an emergency call within two minutes of receiving the call? YES _____ NO _____

7. Does your community have advanced life support units staffed by EMT-paramedics? YES _____ NO _____

8. Are rescue services in your community (EMS, police, fire) provided by well-equipped units staffed by EMTs? YES _____ NO _____

9. Are all emergency services in your community dispatched and coordinated through a central emergency communications center? YES _____ NO _____

10. Is your nearest emergency department staffed on a 24-hour basis by physicians and nurses who are specially trained in emergency medicine? YES _____ NO _____

11. Does your community have a plan to transfer very acutely ill or injured patients to specialty centers? YES _____ NO _____

12. Does your community have an area-wide disaster plan to deal with multi-casualty incidents, natural disasters, and environmental emergencies? YES _____ NO _____

13. Is there one office in charge of the administration, coordination, and evaluation of the EMS system? YES _____ NO _____

Adapted from "A Community Scoring Guide for Emergency Health Services," Office of Emergency Medical Services, The Pennsylvania State University.

Instructions for Emergency Phone Calls

Emergency Phone Numbers

EMS _____ Fire _____ Police _____

Doctor's name _____Number _____

Poison control center _____

Other important numbers:

Name _____ Number _____

Name _____ Number _____

Name _____ Number _____

Name of medical facility with 24-hour emergency care.

_____

Information for Emergency Call (Be prepared to give this information to the EMS dispatcher.)

1. Location

   Street address _____

   City or town _____

   Directions (cross streets, landmarks, etc.)

   _____

2. Phone number from which call is made _____

3. Caller's name _____

4. What happened _____

5. How many injured _____

6. Condition of victim(s) _____

7. Help (first aid) being given _____

Note: Do not hang up first. Let the person you called hang up first.

American Red Cross

When Breathing Stops

1 **Check for Unresponsiveness**

Tap or gently shake victim. Shout, "Are you O.K.?"

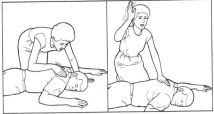

2 **Shout, "Help!"**

Get attention of people who can phone for help.

3 **Position the Victim on His or Her Back**

Roll the victim toward you by pulling slowly and evenly from the victim's hip and shoulder.

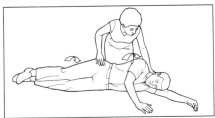

4 **Open the Airway**

Tilt head back and lift chin with fingers under bony part of jaw.

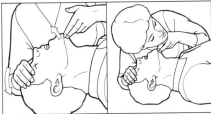

5 **Check for Breathlessness**

Look, listen, and feel for breathing for 3 to 5 seconds.

6 **Give Two Full Breaths**

Keep head tilted back. Pinch nose. Seal your lips tightly around the victim's mouth. Give 2 full breaths for 1 to 1½ seconds each.

7 **Check for Pulse at the Side of the Neck**

Keep head tilted back. Feel for carotid pulse for 5 to 10 seconds.

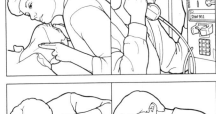

8 **Phone EMS System for Help**

Send someone to call an ambulance. Send 2 people if possible. Give location of emergency and condition of victim.

9 **Begin Rescue Breathing**

Keep head tilted back. Pinch nose. Give 1 breath every 5 seconds. Look, listen, and feel for breathing between breaths.

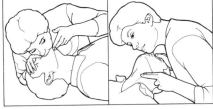

10 **Recheck Pulse Every Minute**

Keep head tilted back. Feel for carotid pulse for 5 to 10 seconds. If victim has pulse but is not breathing, continue rescue breathing.

Local Emergency (EMS) Telephone Number: _____

Everyone should learn how to perform the steps above and how to give CPR. Call your local American Red Cross chapter for information on these techniques and other first aid courses.

American Red Cross

Safety Tips for Swimming

Post these safety tips in any swimming area for all swimmers to read.

- Always swim with companions. Swim only in areas well supervised by lifeguards.
- Never drink alcohol or use drugs when you're swimming or boating.
- Always check the water depth. Walk in from shore or ease in from the dock or the edge of the pool.
- Don't swim if you can't see the bottom of the pool in the deep end, or if the water is cloudy.
- Stay close enough to the shore or pool's edge so you can get to safety by yourself.
- Know the limits of your own swimming abilities. If you're a good swimmer, don't tempt nonswimmers or beginner swimmers to try to keep up with you. Instead, encourage them to stay at a safe depth.
- Watch out for the "dangerous too's"—too tired, too cold, too far from safety, too much sun, too much hard playing.
- Stay out of the water when you're overheated or overtired.
- Keep an eye on younger swimmers at all times.
- Follow the lifeguards' instructions and respect their judgment. Never fake an emergency. Obey all swimming rules.
- Learn the proper way to dive in the water safely. Follow guidelines for safe diving.
- Don't chew gum or eat while you swim. It is dangerous and you could easily choke.
- Wear goggles for surface swimming only, not for underwater swimming.

American Red Cross

Aquatic Agencies

American Camping Association
Bradfordwoods 5000 S.R. 67 N
Martinsville, Indiana 46151-7902
(317) 342-8456

American Canoe Association
8580 Cinderbed Road, Suite 1900
P.O. Box 1190
Newington, Virginia 22122
(703) 550-7523

American Red Cross
17th and D Streets, N.W.
Washington, D C 20006
(202) 737-8300

American Swimming Coaches Association
1 Hall of Fame Drive
Ft. Lauderdale, Florida 33316
(305) 462-6267

Boy Scouts of America
1325 Walnut Hill Lane
Irving, Texas 75038-3096
(214) 659-2000

Council for National Cooperation in Aquatics
901 West New York Street
Indianapolis, Indiana 46223
(317) 638-4238

International Swim and Diving Federation (FINA)
208-3540 West 41st Avenue
Vancouver, British Columbia
Canada V6N3E6

National Collegiate Athletic Association
P.O. Box 1906
Mission, Kansas 66201
(913) 384-3220

National Federation of State High School Associations
11724 Plaza Circle
Box 20626
Kansas City, Missouri 64195
(816) 464-5400

National Safety Council
444 North Michigan Avenue
Chicago, Illinois 60611
(312) 527-4800

National Spa and Pool Institute
2111 Eisenhower Avenue
Alexandria, Virginia 22314
(703) 838-0083

National Swimming Pool Foundation
10803 Gulfdal, Suite 300
San Antonio, Texas 78216
(512) 525-1227

United States Coast Guard
Commandant (G-NAB)
2100 Second Street, S.W.
Washington, D C 20593-0001
(202) 267-1060

United States Coast Guard Auxiliary
3131 Abingdon Street
Arlington, Virginia 22207
(703) 538-4466

United States Diving, Inc.
Pan American Plaza
201 S. Capitol Avenue, Suite 430
Indianapolis, Indiana 46225
(317) 237-5252

United States Swimming, Inc.
1750 East Boulder Street
Colorado Springs, Colorado 80909
(719) 578-4578

United States Synchronized Swimming, Inc.
Pan American Plaza
201 S. Capitol Avenue, Suite 510
Indianapolis, Indiana 46225
(317) 237-5700

United States Water Polo, Inc.
1750 East Boulder Street
Colorado Springs, Colorado 80909
(719) 632-5551

United States Yacht Racing Union
Box 209
Newport, Rhode Island 02840
(401) 849-5200

U.S. Power Squadron
4104 Monument Avenue
Richmond, Virginia 23230
(804) 355-6588

YMCA of the U.S.A.
6083-A Oakbrook Parkway
Norcross, Georgia 30092
(404) 662-5172

YWCA of the U.S.A.
726 Broadway
New York, New York 10003
(212) 614-2700

Glossary

This glossary lists terms and definitions that will be helpful to persons who are interested in water activities and water safety. These terms are found in *Basic Water Safety* and *Emergency Water Safety* textbooks.

Aquatic—Living in or taking place in or on the water.

Aquatic Life—Organisms that live in the water, including plants and animals. Some aquatic life is dangerous to swimmers.

Aquatics—Sports performed in or on the water. Also a professional or career pursuit related to the management and supervision of water-related activities and the operation of facilities (for example, pools, waterfront areas, and other swimming areas that support water-related activities).

Aquatic Director—One who supervises, controls, or manages water-related activities or those areas and facilities that support such activities. (Examples are waterfront director at a lake or summer camp, pool manager, and beach supervisor.)

Asphyxia—Loss of consciousness due to too little oxygen and too much carbon dioxide in the blood. Drowning is death by asphyxiation.

Aspirate—The involuntary breathing of water into the lungs.

Backboard—The rescue device on which a victim of a water-related accident (especially diving) is placed if spinal injury is suspected.

Backwash—An ocean current created as water moves down the slope of a beach under incoming waves, frequently referred to as undertow. Backwash moves straight out, but usually stops when the next wave starts to break. If you are in a backwash, the next wave usually brings you back to shore but not necessarily where you entered.

Bad Ice—Ice that is unsafe for recreation because it is not at least four solid inches thick.

Bailing Device—A container (bucket, scoop, bilge pump, or large sponge) used to remove water from a boat.

Boat Hook—A long pole with a metal hook on one end for reaching lines and objects in the water and maneuvering boats.

Bow—The front part of a boat or other water craft.

Buoyancy—The ability or tendency to float or rise in water.

Capacity Plate—The notice on a boat that indicates the total weight and number of persons allowed on board at one time.

Capsize—When a boat overturns in the water.

Cervical—Related to the neck. (The first seven vertebrae)

Cervical Collar—A device, usually of rigid material, used to immobilize the neck in spinal injury management.

Coccyx—A small, triangular bone at the lower end of the spinal column.

Core Temperature—The deep body temperature, or normal degree of hotness in a human (about 98.6°F, 37°C), usually measured by a rectal thermometer.

CPR—Cardiopulmonary resuscitation. CPR is performed only when a victim has no pulse or breathing and should be done only by someone who is trained in the procedure.

Cramp—A sudden, painful, involuntary contraction of a muscle, usually because of fatigue, a chill, or strain.

Current—A body of water flowing in a definite direction. Currents are dangerous to swimmers because currents can carry swimmers great distances, often before they realize it. Especially dangerous currents include river rapids, river hydraulics, and ocean currents.

Debark—To go ashore from a ship or boat.

Distressed Swimmer—A person who is unable to get to safety without assistance, but is able to keep afloat and breathe and may be able to call for help. A person in distress can soon tire and become a drowning person.

Diver's Flag—A red, rectangular flag with a diagonal white stripe that underwater divers fly from their boats or floats to warn craft in the area that they are below the surface. The flag on a staff should be at least three feet above the surface, and all divers should stay within 100 feet of the flag.

Glossary

Drift—A side current (littoral) in the ocean or gulf that moves parallel to shore. Drifts are caused by waves approaching shore from side to side; drifts can carry swimmers down the beach from where they entered the water.

Drowning—Death by asphyxiation or loss of consciousness as a result of too little oxygen and too much carbon dioxide in the blood. If water is inhaled, death can result.

Drowning Person—A person who is unable to keep afloat or get air or call for help. The victim may be passive (floating facedown or just under the surface) or active (desperately trying to stay above the water and get air).

Embark—To go on board a ship or boat.

Emergency Action Plan—A predetermined plan for responding to water accidents. Every plan should include an emergency signal, safety equipment, and emergency procedures.

EMS—Emergency medical services (EMS) system to contact such services as ambulances, rescue squads, fire departments or police. The EMS may be activated in many communities by dialing 911 on the telephone. Look in your local telephone directory for the emergency telephone number in your community.

Exhaustion—In this text, exhaustion means that a person no longer has the energy to make progress through the water or to float. It can occur as a reaction to cold water, excessive sunbathing, fatigue, or too much water activity.

Fins—Flexible, rubber or silicone, shoe-like devices worn by swimmers for added enjoyment and underwater exploration, and by lifeguards for rescue and recovery.

First Aid—Emergency care of a sick or injured person until trained medical professionals can assist.

Flange—The slightly flared end of a snorkel that goes between a person's lips and teeth.

Flotation Device—A buoyant device that swimmers and nonswimmers can either wear or hold onto in deep water to keep their heads above water.

Gale Warnings—A meterological warning that strong winds—ranging in speed from 32 to 63 miles per hour—are possible in a particular area.

Gasp Reflex—A spasm of the larynx (upper part of the respiratory tract) resulting in the closing of a person's airway. This reflex spasm may occur right after a person plunges into water, particularly if the water is cold. Drowning may occur if a victim is unable to maintain his or her face above water.

Good Ice—Ice that is at least four solid inches thick and safe for recreation.

Gunwale—The upper edge of the side of a ship or boat.

Hazard—A potential source of danger.

Heat Exhaustion—A physical condition caused by too much time in the sun. Its symptoms include cool, pale, and moist skin; heavy sweating; headache; nausea; dizziness; and vomiting. Medical attention may be required.

Heat Stroke—Similar to heat exhaustion in that it is caused by too much exposure to the sun. It should be treated as a life-threatening emergency. Symptoms include hot, red skin; shock or unconsciousness; and very high body temperature.

Heaving Line—An emergency device that can be thrown to a victim to grasp and be pulled to safety. The line should float and should be white, yellow, or another highly visible color. A weighted object on the throwing end gives the throw more accuracy.

H.E.L.P.—Heat Escape Lessening Posture. A body position that can help a person reduce heat loss when in cold water.

Huddle—A body position for two or more persons in cold water to help reduce heat loss.

Hydraulic—A vertical whirlpool current that is created as water flows over an object (a fallen tree or a low-head dam, for example). Some hydraulics are strong enough to keep swimmers and even boats in the whirlpool.

Hyperventilation—Repeated deep breathing, used by some people to try to increase their breath-holding time. Excessive "blowing off" of carbon dioxide can interfere with your body's normal signals to take breaths. If you hyperventilate and swim underwater, you could pass out.

Hypothermia—A condition of low body temperature, where there is a drop of three to four degrees from the normal core or deep-body temperature. If uncorrected, hypothermia can lead to death. Exposure to cold water is one cause of temperature drop.

Ice Cross—An ice-rescue device made in the shape of a cross that, when pushed over the ice to a person who has fallen through the ice, spreads the weight over a wide area and helps prevent the ice from breaking while the victim is dragged to safety.

Immersion—Being completely covered by water, being submerged in water, or being plunged into water.

Immobile—Motionless. A person who has a suspected spinal injury should be kept immobile until emergency medical personnel arrive.

In-Line Stabilization—A technique for immobilizing a victim's head, neck, and back with the rescuer's hands when a spinal injury is suspected.

Intervertebral Disks—Cushions of cartilage that separate the vertebrae of the spinal cord.

Larynx—The structure of muscle and cartilage at the upper end of the trachea. The larynx contains the vocal cords. See **Gasp Reflex.**

Lemon—An oblong object, usually made of cellular foam or rubber, attached to the end of the line on a ring buoy to prevent the line from slipping when the ring buoy is thrown.

Lifeguard—A well-trained, certified, employed aquatic professional and rescuer whose primary responsibility is to assure the safety of the people using a water facility.

Littoral—See **Drift.**

Low-Head Dam—A manufactured structure at or just below the surface of a river. When water flows over a low-head dam, a dangerous hydraulic current is often created, possibly trapping boats and canoes.

Mask—A device that underwater divers wear over their eyes and nose to see clearly underwater.

Modified Jaw Thrust—A method of opening the airway that minimizes movement of the head and neck. While positioned behind the victim's head, the rescuer places his or her hands on both sides of the victim's head, and applies pressure to the angles of the lower jaw with the fingers to lift the jaw upwards. At the same time, the palms of the rescuer's hands keep the victim's head from moving backwards.

Navigation Rules—Rules established by a committee appointed by the U.S. Congress and administered by the U.S. Coast Guard. These rules are also known as the "rules of the road" and are designed to keep boating safe and enjoyable. The rules regulate such boating issues as right of way, meeting, crossing, and passing, among others.

Panic—A sudden, overwhelming terror that can prevent you from helping yourself or someone else. It can occur in most water accidents.

PFD—Personal Flotation Device. PFDs include life preservers, buoyant vests, buoyant cushions, and special purpose devices for water recreation. The Coast Guard has approved specific types of PFDs.

Pike Surface Dive—A method of submerging in the water in which the swimmer first bends at the waist and then lifts the legs above the head to provide momentum down into the water.

Recommendation—In this text, a suggested specification or requirement (for example, recommendations for safe diving) from expert evaluations and opinions.

Rescue Breathing—The act of performing artificial respiration when the victim of a water emergency cannot breathe alone. Rescue breathing can be done in or out of the water.

Rescue Tube—A vinyl, foam tube about three inches by six inches by forty inches, with a six-foot tow line and web shoulder strap. It can be used to help a victim who is within six to eight feet of shore. It is often used by lifeguards when making swimming rescues.

Ring Buoy—A rescue device made of cork, kapok, cellular foam, or plastic-covered material that keeps a person afloat.

Rip—An ocean current that moves straight out to sea beyond wave break areas. Rip currents can move swimmers into deep water and are a major cause of surf emergencies.

Glossary

Sacrum—Fused vertebrae of the lower back below the lumbar region and above the coccyx.

Schooling Fish—A large number of fish of one kind swimming together. Schooling fish weaken ice formations and can make ice unsafe for recreation.

Sculling—A method of using your hands and arms to propel or support yourself in the water.

Seizure—A sudden attack. Medical emergencies such as seizures are a leading cause of drowning and dangerous water-related accidents.

Shepherd's Crook—A long pole with a hook on the end that can be used to either pull a conscious drowning person to safety or to encircle a submerged drowning person and pull the victim to the water's surface.

Small Craft—Boats and canoes that are 16 feet or less in length. The U.S. Coast Guard has a detailed classification system for all types of small and large boats.

Snorkel—Usually a J-shaped rubber breathing device, 12 to 15 inches long, that extends just above the surface of the water to allow a person to breathe when swimming with the face in the water.

Snorkel Keeper—A small device on the side of a mask that secures the snorkel to the mask and keeps the snorkel at the correct angle.

Spine—A strong, flexible column that supports the head and trunk. It encloses and provides protection to the spinal cord of the nervous system. It consists of small bones (vertebrae) separated from each other by cushions of cartilage tissue (disks). It comprises five regions: the cervical or neck region, the thoracic or midback region, the lumbar or lower back region, the sacrum, and the coccyx.

Standards—In this text, standards are water safety specifications or requirements, usually authorized by reputable organizations and sources.

Stern—The rear end of a ship or boat.

Submerge—To place or plunge under water.

Sudden Immersion—An unplanned entry into water by a person who, for example, has accidently fallen off a bridge, or pier, or boat, or who has waded off an unexpected drop-off in the water.

Survival Floating—A resting position while floating facedown in warm water.

Thoracic Region—The part of the body between the neck and the diaphragm; the chest or mid-back region.

Tired Swimmer—A swimmer who is too tired to get to shore or poolside but is not in immediate danger.

Treading Water—Maintaining a near-vertical position in the water by using the arms and legs to propel or support the body and keep the head above water level.

Trimming—Balancing the weight on a boat from side to side and front to back.

Undertow—See **Backwash**.

Vertebrae—The small bones that make up the spine. The vertebrae are separated from each other by cushions of cartilage called disks.

Warning Flag—A flag indicating potentially dangerous swimming conditions, for example, a yellow flag indicates that caution is needed, and a red flag indicates that swimming is prohibited.

Water Safety Instructor—A well-trained swimming instructor who possesses knowledge and skill relating to personal safety in, on, or around water, and who is certified by the American Red Cross.

Wave—A general word for a curving ridge or swell in the surface of the ocean or other body of water.

Winging—A motion with the hands and arms when floating on the back to propel the swimmer.

Index

Index

Notes

Notes

Notes

Notes

Notes

Notes